To STACEY
and EddY

FEARLESS
WISDOM

June 2, 2022

I thank the universe for bringing you and Eddy into my world on a gorgeous day on the beach in the Turks and Caicos. I love how the universe works and always bringing like-minded people together.

I wanted you to have a copy of the first book in the Fear-clearing Trilogy I have written.

Thanks again for the Secret as I had not previously been aware of it.

Talk Soon

PRAISE FOR RICHARD A. FELLER

"I love who Richard is, a kind, strong, gentle, loving, and wise man. I also love the way he writes because even though I don't have a college degree he brings the depth of his knowledge down to earth and makes it simple to understand and apply. It is also a fun read. Personally, I live my life according to these principles and I know they work. They will also work for you, even if at first, they may seem strange or weird."

—Kay Crawford, *wife, mother, Health Therapist and Nutritionist*

"Richard Feller brings a lifetime of growing in wisdom to this book. Regardless of where you are on your journey, you will find bits of encouragement and opportunities to move past the fears that limit you. You will discover important questions and issues to explore in the text and in the exercises. Let this search be a springboard of new learning for you."

—G. H., Ph.D., *consultant, business owner, and university professor*

"I am so pleased to highly recommend this book to readers. When it comes to metaphysical subjects, Richard Feller has a grasp unlike any I have even seen. To faithfully read his words, to follow his instructions and do the exercises contained within is to begin to go down a true path of enlightenment and eventual success. The impressive depth and breadth of his background, both in the spiritual and business world, has set the conditions to place him at the top of those who teach such skills. Get his book, make it your own, and find yourself well grounded in having the universe work on your behalf."

—Jeff McCrehan, *former speech writer for Robert Mueller when he was the Director of the FBI, speech writer for the FBI, and journalist*

BOOK #1 OF THE
"FEAR-CLEARING" TRILOGY

3 ancient
secret keys
revealed to
clear your
fears

FEARLESS
WISDOM

Transform your life through
transcendence and a divine
spiritual shift

Richard A. Feller, MA, MBA, Ph.D.
FOREWORD BY ALAN COHEN

ISBN: 978-1-957926-00-1 (paperback)

ISBN: 978-1-957926-02-5 (hardcover)

ISBN: 978-1-957926-01-8 (eBook)

I dedicate this book to my Creative Source,
the One who is the Source of everything good in my life;
and to all those who have had the courage to learn to
surmount their fears so they could walk their divine
path of perfection and unlimited wisdom
here in earth.

CONTENTS

15 | FOREWORD

19 | ABOUT THE AUTHOR

21 | INTRODUCTION

27 | WHAT IS METAPHYSICS OR SPIRITUALITY?

33 | CHAPTER 1
WHAT IS FEAR?

41 | CHAPTER 2
TRANSFORM YOUR FEARS INTO FAITH

49 | CHAPTER 3
A NEW PARADIGM: RECOGNIZING YOUR COMPLETENESS

63 | CHAPTER 4

THE MORE FEARS YOU REMOVE – THE MORE YOU WILL RELEASE YOUR INNER MAGNIFICENCE

71 | CHAPTER 5

WE TEMPORARILY WALK ON EARTH WITH A HUMAN BODY

79 | CHAPTER 6

WE BEGIN THIS LIFE WITH LESSONS FROM PRIOR LIVES

91 | CHAPTER 7

IDENTIFYING FEARS AND STRENGTHS FROM PRIOR LIVES

105 | CHAPTER 8

YOU HAVE CONTINUED TO GROW YOUR FEARS AND YOUR STRENGTHS WHILE YOU HAVE BEEN HERE ON EARTH

129 | CHAPTER 9

TRANSFORM YOURSELF

145 | CHAPTER 10
TWO DIVERGENT ROADS

159 | CHAPTER 11
WE ARE FORTUNATE TO BE LIVING ON EARTH NOW

167 | CHAPTER 12
WE ARE LIVING IN A WORLD OF INCREASING CHANGE

181 | CHAPTER 13
THREE PREVIOUSLY SECRET KEYS TO REMOVE YOUR FEARS

193 | CHAPTER 14
GOD IS PERFECT, IS UNFATHOMABLE WISDOM, AND IS ETERNAL LOVE

205 | CHAPTER 15
MAN IS A PERFECT SOUL, AS ARE ALL FORMS OF LIFE ON EARTH

213 | CHAPTER 16
YOU ARE PERFECT, SPIRITUAL AND DIVINE; AND YOU ARE IN THE PROCESS OF REALIZING IT

229 | CHAPTER 17
USE THE KEYS TO RELEASE YOUR FEARS

241 | CHAPTER 18
USING KEY NUMBER ONE

265 | CHAPTER 19
USING KEY NUMBER TWO

299 | CHAPTER 20
USING KEY NUMBER THREE

333 | CHAPTER 21
YOU NOW HAVE THE KNOWLEDGE TO CLEAR ALL YOUR FEARS

341 | **ACKNOWLEDGMENTS**

345 | **OTHER BOOKS BY THE AUTHOR**

359 | **ADDITIONAL SERVICES**

TABLE OF EXERCISES

54 | EXERCISE 1
How do you React to Learning
Something New?

94 | EXERCISE 2
Your List of Influencers

95 | EXERCISE 3
Your Earth Circumstances – Your
Fears and Limitations

98 | EXERCISE 4
Your Earth Circumstances – Your
Strengths and Assets

112 | EXERCISE 5
If You have a Challenge with
Prosperity

125 | EXERCISE 6
Fears and Limitations You have
Kept and Added to as an Adult

126 | EXERCISE 7
Strengths You have kept, Expanded,
and Added as an Adult

152 | EXERCISE 8
Who and What is God to You Today?

153 | EXERCISE 9
Who is the God to those People who Surround You?

162 | EXERCISE 10
How do You React to Change?

174 | EXERCISE 11
How Are You Reacting to Covid?

186 | EXERCISE 12
What is Your Initial Reaction to the Three Keys?

232 | EXERCISE 13
Take One of Your Fears and Analyze it

232 | EXERCISE 14
If You Select Key One – Perfect God

235 | EXERCISE 15
If You Select Key Two – Perfect Man

236 | EXERCISE 16
If You Select Key Three – Perfect Me

FOREWORD

by Allan Cohen

We are living during extraordinary times. The world has experienced unprecedented challenges and changes in a short period of time. As a result, we have had to pivot quickly, think beyond traditional patterns and practices, and come up with far-reaching, more holistic solutions. We must probe deeper into our attitudes, beliefs, visions, and strategies. Innovation demands greater honesty and reliance on our authentic self. While this process is not always easy or comfortable, self-introspection, honest communication, and reaching for higher answers provide more effective long-term solutions rather than adhering to short-term Band-Aids.

As a sign on a highway road construction stated, "The inconvenience is temporary. The improvement is permanent."

I have had the pleasure to call Richard Feller my friend for many years. I used to co-teach with his late wife Carla Gordan, one of the most gifted trance mediums I have ever known. Her intuitive personal guidance helped me in more ways than I can express. I have described in depth Carla's work with nonphysical guides in my most recent book, *Friends in High Places.*

I am delighted that Richard has finally decided to share his vast knowledge of business, education, administration, spirituality and metaphysics. I commend him for his courage to come forth and introduce the element of spiritual awareness into the marketplace. He has an unbelievably fascinating and varied background, including successfully navigating seven different careers while now entering his eighth as an author. He has been an executive with two of the largest corporations in the world, as well as other businesses where he served as the CEO. In those roles, he helped to bring transformation to the business world as he successfully navigated the waters of change.

Richard has shared his knowledge in this remarkable book about the incredible destructive role fear plays in our lives as it imprisons our mental and thinking faculties while concurrently destroying our self-confidence and self-esteem. He expands upon this theme and illuminates the importance of removing fear, regardless of whether in our personal lives or in a business setting. Richard articulates how the world has attempted to convince us that fear is real and not founded in illusion. As his book analyzes and examines fear, and its associated false concepts, you will recognize how fear has been used to control your beliefs and limit your thoughts while shackling and enslaving you; decreasing your self-love and self-esteem; while limiting how you think and function.

Yet all of our fears lead us to learn how we can grow beyond them. In this book you will be guided to remove your fears and return to your roots of spiritual freedom. You will discover that you possess greater personal power and strength than you have ever known possible. While you will enhance your capacity to thrive in business, even more fundamentally, you will enhance your capacity to thrive in relationships, health, and any other area of your life that is meaningful to you.

Due to the importance of this subject, Richard has been inspired by his nonphysical spiritual teachers to write a trilogy on fear-clearing. This is the first book in that series.

I am excited for the life-changing information you are about to receive. This book contains the answers to not just business challenges, but to the many questions we all have about how to live a rewarding, soul-fulfilling, and successful life. I wish you well on your great adventure.

ALAN COHEN

Alan Cohen is one of the most popular inspirational writers and speakers in America and his books, tapes, and seminars have touched millions. He is the best-selling author of thirty inspirational books including the best-selling *A Course in Miracles Made Easy*, and the award-winning *A Deep Breath of Life.* He is a contributing writer for the #1 New York Times best-selling series *Chicken Soup for the Soul* which has sold more than 500 million copies. His work has been featured in *Oprah.com*, *USA Today*, the *Washington Post*, *Huffington Post*, and many other magazines. Alan's work has been translated into 31 foreign languages.

ABOUT THE AUTHOR

RICHARD A. FELLER

Richard is an internationally acclaimed business executive who brings a unique and innovative blend of experience and background to the spiritual world. He has been an administrator and faculty member at two state universities; a dean; administrator responsible for services to 50,000 senior citizens; a minister, therapist, and healer; an executive responsible for organization change, management development, succession planning, and economic turn arounds at the 50th and 200th largest corporations in the world; as well as being a CEO with several highly diverse businesses including his own. He has successfully reinvented himself within 7 different careers.

Dr. Feller holds an MA, MBA, and Ph.D. Numerous post-graduate degrees/certifications augment his background including economics, value engineering, marketing, real estate, psychology, and the ministry. He has been highly spiritual since he was a teenager.

Dr. Feller is a business visionary and business strategist. He is comfortable working with various cultures and nationalities since he has worked in twelve different countries in his career.

He lives in the Washington, D.C. area and the Turks and Caicos with his wife Susan.

INTRODUCTION

My objective with this first book of our trilogy to clear fear is to *send you off on a journey that transforms your life.*

I truly want you to become more self-confident, happier, healthier, more abundant, involved in creating increasingly loving relationships, and being more self-aware than you have ever imagined possible.

I want you to learn that you can become responsible for creating and controlling your own destiny and not continue to be plummeted randomly about whenever the winds of earth choose to blow in a different direction.

I want you to feel good about yourself and to be excited about the life you are living.

I want you to wake up excited each morning, thrilled to be alive, and enthusiastically welcome your new day and all of the wonderful thing's life is about to bring you.

This is why the subject of fear and the release of fear is so important. Until you become aware of, and begin to clear your fears, you will continue to live the same existence that you are currently living. You will continue to attract more and more fear instead of what you are really seeking.

You will discover in this book that life is a proportional relationship: The more fears you release, the more you will unleash the incredible power that the universe has placed at your disposal; simply waiting for you to maximize your use of this energy and its unlimited capacity.

Every single one of us has phenomenal and unimagined capabilities at our disposal. For example, we have an average of *86 billion neurons in our human brain alone.* 86 billion!

That is nearly one half of all the number of stars in the Milky Way.

Unfortunately, we use but a minor fraction of what the universe has made available to us while we allow the remainder to go unharvested, to simply stagnate and rot in the field.

This book is designed to help you change this paradigm as it assists you to take back control of your own destiny, so you can create what you want to achieve, while living here in earth.

You will learn that you have the ability to manifest whatever you want to create in your world through your focused thoughts and inspired actions.

This may include a new and exciting fun job rather than continuing to work in a position filled with drudgery.

It may include learning new knowledge and skills to allow you to function more effectively as a manager of people in a rapidly changing environment.

It may include expanding your innovativeness, and creating a new business, or even a new job, one where you feel excited, worthy and fulfilled.

It may include acquiring self-confidence and personal self-esteem, rather than continuing to experience the misery of not being able to make decisions, or suffering indecision when you are forced into making a decision.

It may include gaining prosperity versus barely having enough to get by with each paycheck and being forced to make decisions between medicine, food, and rent.

It may mean attracting a new car rather than getting by with one that barely gets you where you want to go.

Or, it may mean that you transform yourself into a powerful, gentle being, in contrast to an individual who walks around with feelings of suppressed anger lurking beneath the surface ready to explode outwardly on a whim.

All of these things will become possible in your world as you learn to clear your fears, focus your thoughts, acquire the correspondence between you and that which you want to create; and then allow your desires, your requests, to manifest.

What we will be teaching you in this book may initially appear to be magic or perhaps even somewhat weird. However, I assure you it isn't. Instead, you will be learning about the natural laws of the universe, together with their profound unlimitedness.

You will not only learn their incredible power, but you will also learn how you, with your unlimited inner being, your core, can personally access this power because your Creative Source has placed it all at your disposal. Best of all - it is absolutely free!

In other words, you will learn, going forward, how to - *make the impossible - possible.*

You will discover these learnings to be true regardless of whether you work in the business world, in another profession, or if you are a live-at-home mom or dad. You will also find there is no difference in terms of learning how to create your dreams and aspirations regardless of what they may be.

Bottom-line, we are all people, human beings, regardless of where we work, what we do, or how we think. The principles and knowledge shared in this book are applicable to everyone, everywhere, throughout existence.

When we do not utilize our inner unlimitedness, when we block it with our fears from fully expressing, we leave much of who and what we are to stagnate and not blossom into what it could become.

This book will link you with the aspects of the universe that Aristotle in ancient Greece espoused through his work with metaphysics - which is not religious. It will then advance his teachings. Together, we will explore your unlimited inner magnificence, your internal voice, while bringing you in touch with the natural laws that govern the galaxies.

This may be new knowledge that you will be hearing for the first time since it has not been widely disseminated.

It may also at first seem strange, because it is likely you have only been taught and learned what earth wants you to know. I know, for example, that these learnings were not available or discussed in the educational, business, or administrative worlds I navigated. That does not make them less true.

As a matter of fact, anyone who would have discussed with another that they had been thinking about a friend, and then they received a phone call from that person; or that that they had received some uncanny sign from a loved one who had passed on; or that they had a dream and then it happened; would have been laughed at forty years ago.

Today, even that paranoia has changed as more than 66 million Americans are saying they are "spiritual but not necessarily religious" as they search for answers which have eluded them. Similarly, metaphysical and inspirational sayings are appearing in everyday life, including greeting cards, as well as in spiritually oriented television statement pages and programs.

In this book, you will learn that you are far more than simply someone who is occupying a physical body living a mundane earth existence. Instead, you will discover we are spiritual beings who temporarily occupy a human body while we experience the lessons of earth rather than a human who is attempting to be spiritual.

For those of you who are not acquainted with this knowledge, it may seem different, but it will also be transformative in that it will provide answers to unanswered questions. For those of you who are interested in applying these principles with your business, or with your family as well as yourself, you will find them to be profoundly helpful. For those of you who already have a familiarity with these teachings, the knowledge in this book will assist you take your next steps in growth.

The wisdom in this book is applicable to everyone who lives on earth regardless of what field of employment they have chosen, whether they are young or old, married or single, children or childless, and whether they are or are not religious.

The more you learn about yourself and the incredible power that you have, the more you will be in a position to confidently navigate the world of change you are currently facing which will only accelerate even more in the future until it touches every single facet of your life.

The knowledge in this book has also been designed to allow you to steady your ship, so you can navigate your own waters of change in the future, no matter what directions the storms may attempt to blow you in.

It will also provide you with the opportunity to transform yourself through transcendence and a divine spiritual shift.

WHAT IS METAPHYSICS OR SPIRITUALITY?

Many are confused about what spirituality, or metaphysics, means. So, I thought it beneficial to provide a definition at the very beginning, since I have integrated metaphysical and spiritual principles throughout the book, together with learnings from business, education, administration, and psychology. I believe that metaphysics and spirituality are very closely aligned and this is the reason I have chosen to use the same overall definition for each and use them both interchangeably.

I believe that the principles of metaphysics/spirituality are as valuable in the business or work world as they are in our families or any other aspects of our life, despite metaphysics or spirituality not being words traditionally used in those settings.

Spirituality or metaphysics involves a *feeling*, a *perception*, a *belief* that there is something greater than yourself, that there is something more to being human than simply the sensory experiences of touch, sight, smell, taste and hearing.

It is like when you *feel* something is about to occur and then it does; or you dream something which then takes place; or when you experience something you feel has already happened. We have even developed a name for it and we call it *de-ja vu*.

Every one of us has had these types of experiences occur, some many, many times, although they are seldom openly discussed.

Metaphysics, which to many had its origin in ancient Greece with Aristotle and Parmenides around 475 BC, is a sense that there is a greatness, an order to everything that exists; that the whole of existence is divine or cosmic in nature, and that somehow, someway, *we are a part of all that exists.*

Metaphysics/spirituality *is not a religion* any more than quantum physics or mathematics is, and does not involve a gigantic white man with a long flowing beard sitting on a throne somewhere in the sky.

Rather, spirituality means an *inner knowing,* or perception that your life has significance in a context beyond a mundane everyday existence at the level of biological needs.

Acquiring the knowledge that your life has significance means coming to an awareness that each of us is a significant part of a purposeful unfolding of life in our universe, and that there is a *purpose* to our life. It is also why the vast majority of people intuitively, somehow, *know that* a part of us will exist after the time of our so-called earth death.

It explains the features of reality that exist beyond the physical world and our immediate five senses. It seeks to understand the invisible, spiritual nature of all life which *transcends* the physical or material plane in which we live.

While some define spirituality as only being concerned about the human spirit or soul in opposition to material or physical things, I take a much larger and more inclusive definition and believe that metaphysics/spirituality involves exploring such universal themes as love, fear, power, growth, guilt, violence, self-confidence, compassion, life after death, inspiration, birth, health, prosperity/abundance, wisdom, and truth; all of which are both divine and material, because they reflect who and what we are.

Spirituality/metaphysics involves an exploration of how we can learn to release the inner unlimitedness we have at our disposal; like highly enlightened individuals have done throughout history; so, we can attempt to replicate or surpass their inspirational example, as they taught.

It provides us with the stimulus to learn why Jesus who was spiritual but not religious made the statements, "You can do greater things than I have done", and, "It is done unto you as you believe." These principles are becoming increasingly essential in our everyday life as dramatic changes take place all around us; regardless of whether it is in becoming personally more self-aware and sensitive, enhancing the quality of your family life, or transcendence in a rapidly changing business and work world environment.

It involves gaining the knowledge that universal energy can be transformed through our focused thoughts and actions into substance and form. It provides the awareness that we are truly one with all existence.

Spirituality/metaphysics involves understanding yourself at a deeper level than you have likely ever previously explored. It means discovering your unlimited inner nature, and then learning how to express it in your beliefs, thoughts and actions.

It involves gaining the knowledge that you are a spiritual being temporarily occupying a human body instead of a human being attempting to become spiritual; and that there are universal spiritual laws governing the universe which you can have work to your benefit instead of working against you.

Spirituality involves self-healing and personal growth so you can learn, achieve, and express such positive attributes as self-love, self-confidence, abundance, self-esteem, health, and loving relationships; together with developing an ever-expanding capacity for love and generosity so you may be of increasing service to yourself and others.

A trend in modern society is that many are leaving formalized religion and are transitioning into spirituality to search for the answers that they believe have eluded them in formalized religion.

A person can practice spirituality/metaphysics and belong to a formalized religion.

Or, they can practice spirituality/metaphysics without belonging to a formalized religion.

Some do one or the other, some do both. Neither is right or wrong. It is simply what is right for that individual.

This is why 66 million Americans, or 20% of the population in the United States today say they are spiritual, but not necessarily religious.

On a personal basis, the importance of spirituality/metaphysics is that it helps me to explore, discover, and be in a better position to express my unlimitedness, my divinity, in action and in service.

I hope it does the same for you.

△

WHAT IS FEAR?

"President Franklin Delano Roosevelt told the American people on the advent of World War II, "There is nothing to fear - but fear itself".

No truer words have ever been spoken. The "fear of fear!"

Yet, in our busy lives, we don't generally think about fear, or even consider what it is.

The truth is that Fear is infectious. It is highly contagious. It comes in many different currencies and denominations. In terms of healthcare alone, it is the number one killer, although we call it by different names, such as heart disease, cancer, stress or tension.

It seems as if every newspaper headline, or television news report, brings us face-to-face with another fear-aroused problem.

For instance, Covid, a change so massive and global in nature that none of us, even those in the field of change, could have envisioned such a possibility taking place so quickly even a few years ago. Yet it occurred while we were active participants, right in front of our eyes, instantaneously, in 190 countries, while bringing massive and devastating illness with more than one million deaths in the United States alone. Concurrently, it made real the fear of the potential collapse of our financial system, business closures, loss of jobs, supply chain issues, and isolation. Even though our politicians like to try and tell us the end is near, the ramifications will be ongoing and impactful for years.

Some have even called Covid the *Fear Pandemic* since it continues to fearfully disrupt every single facet of our life while forcing us to deeply question aspects of life, we were previously not willing or anxious to face or discuss: Death, what happens after death, whether or not to fully isolate or take the vaccine, loss of freedom, personal values, spirituality, the relevancy of work and its purpose, mental illness, domestic violence, and suicide.

Additional fears evolve around inflation; a pending recession or depression; home evictions and foreclosures; pension and savings plan erosion; mammoth student debt; escalating prices; supply chain shortages; inflation; terrorism attacks; mass shootings; protests; political disagreements; violence; riots; new wars between Russia and Ukraine; increased frequency of earthquakes, hurricanes, volcanoes and tornados; oil leaks; and the highest divorce, societal violence, and murder rates in history.

Each of these experiences has come into our daily lives, uninvited. They have become what we now call the *"New Normal"*.

Each of these incidences are fear in one form or another. We each face these types of fears in our daily existence - either directly or as a ripple effect from other occurrences – yet we call them by names other than fear. Accordingly, fear becomes camouflaged as something else and it escapes our immediate attention.

Fear comes in many different forms. These include stress, anxiety, depression, panic attacks and disease.

In reality, *fear is the taproot underlying illness and all limitations.*

Fear strips our strength and erodes our self-confidence. It quickly transitions a "natural positive life outlook" - into a negative energy where we *"feel lesser than everyone and everything else."* We anxiously brace ourselves for the next "fearful episode" to strike, even though we don't know what it may be.

While impacting us emotionally, mentally, and psychologically, fear also destroys the physical bodies we wear by striking our adrenal glands, heart, respiratory system, stomach, and kidneys; creating heart attacks, diabetes and cancer. This is why stress-induced problems are the number one health problem or killer today.

Sometimes fears are so small they simply appear to be annoyances. However, fear causes stress and tension regardless of size or magnitude. Most of us are so accustomed to living with and accepting stress in our daily lives, that new fears are simply accepted as a normal part of our existence/living.

After a quick knee-jerk reaction, we absorb the new fear symptoms, and try to continue on from there. Our tendency is to *pretend* that fears, anxieties, and stress, are just a part of normal life instead of taking the time to deal with them and to clear, or heal them – that is if we even give ourselves any time whatsoever - to think about them at all.

Over time we have adapted, and have become *masters of self-denial, and simply absorb the new fears*; while the negative toll on our minds and physical bodies grows exponentially, all while being "supposedly invisible".

However, our *Big Fears* vividly contrast with *smaller* fears. *Big fears* occur when you have a situation jump into your world so fast, and without warning, that it hits you squarely between the eyes: Like someone unexpectedly sneaks up behind you and hits you over the head with a baseball bat!

Big fears completely shake your world! *They* are just plain *too big, too bad, too powerful,* to try to ignore and pretend they don't exist.

They grab your full attention with everything they've got, and they shake every single fiber of your being *until they get your full and immediate attention*!

Examples include a sudden job loss, not enough money to pay your rent, an inability to pay for both food and medication, an eviction, a divorce, a sudden unexpected illness or death.

When fear strikes suddenly - like this - it is *devastating!*

It is so scary *it stops you dead in your tracks.*

It's like a sharp slap in the face.

It is demonizing.

Your adenine starts pumping.

Your mind goes into panic mode.

You stop thinking and functioning well.

You begin to become paranoid, and withdraw from the world.

You become depressed.

You want to stay in bed longer and longer.

You attempt to sleep more, but instead, find yourself waking up, often abruptly, opening your eyes to find that you are drenched in sweat.

Your chest hurts.

Your breathing is labored.

You become gun shy.

You begin to anxiously prepare, subconsciously, for the next destructive thing to pop up out of nowhere – and – *add to your misery!*

Your emotions become increasingly destructive. You judge and criticize yourself more frequently. Your self-confidence takes a beating. Your self-esteem wanes.

You alternate between feeling sorry for yourself, seeing yourself as a victim, and beating yourself up.

As your fear level builds, you may come close to tears; or at least, you *feel those tears,* even if you may refuse to allow the outside world to physically see them.

Your thinking becomes hazy, and it lacks the clarity you previously enjoyed.

Your world, as you have known it, begins to crumple, and *you start to lose sight of whom and what you really are – the real you, the inner, Divine You.*

This is the destructive power of fear, and how it strips you of your natural power!

Your physical body, trying to function under this enormous stress and tension, begins to disintegrate as fearful situations continue to escalate.

Your blood pressure goes sky high.

It feels difficult to take another breath.

You feel suffocated.

It is as if someone grabs you around your throat and begins to squeeze the life out of you.

Your chest hurts.

Your stomach feels like it is tied up in knots.

Your self-confidence continues to erode.

It feels as if your entire world is crumbling, and you, along with it.

Chemicals in your body no longer interact as effectively as they once did. Your adrenal glands release more and more adrenaline. As a result, you begin to experience headaches, panic attacks, insulin/ diabetic shock, migraines, gout, anxiety, anxiety attacks, and/or pre-cancer symptoms.

You become more and more like a zombie going through the daily motions of life – as if you are in a daze.

You feel like curling up in a fetal position, going to bed, and never waking up. Depression and suicidal thoughts become your new norm.

Your positive self-perception is gone. Prayer is forgotten, God is forgotten.

Everything is now prey to your fear-laden, paralyzing situation.

Now, this is what fear is, as it takes over your life, and your existence!

This kind of fear is actually *touchable* for those of us who have experienced it. It is like a strong negative vibration. It is so real – you can practically *see it,* touch it, *feel it.*

All of us have experienced some, or all, of these symptoms. For most of us, we have experienced them, *many, many times*!

While bigger fears are more intensively dramatic than smaller ones, the spiritual truth is that *all fear, regardless of size or intensity, causes* profound damage: Physically, emotionally, mentally, psychologically and spiritually.

It is not a question of whether we have been impacted by unwarranted fear. The reality is: We all have – and are - continually!

Fear is like a *"blanket that we create"* and then wrap around ourselves. It serves to push us down, not upward. It functions to suffocate our aspirations, our desires, *our belief in who and what we truly are - and what we can become.*

It stifles us from expressing the inner magic of our creation and the unlimitedness we are.

The thicker this blanket of fear becomes, the less we have the ability to express who we already are.

THE QUESTION BECOMES: WHAT DO WE CHOOSE TO DO ABOUT IT?

TRANSFORM YOUR FEARS
INTO FAITH

"Unwarranted fear has assumed a power over us that it holds over no other creature on earth. It need not be this way".

—Gavin De Becke

This is the purpose of the book:

1. To assist you to better understand fear, what it is, and the negative impact fear and its symptoms have on each of us

2. To provide you with tools so *you* can begin to learn how to effectively manage your fears

3. To use this knowledge to not only transform yourself, but also to be of service to those with whom you come into contact in your everyday life regardless of whether they are family, friends, employees, or work colleagues, and

4. Most importantly, to help you *learn how to transform your fears into love and faith – SO YOU CAN BECOME THE GREATER VERSION OF YOURSELF*

None of us, no matter how fearful our current circumstances may seem to be, have to continue to allow our fears to disrupt, cripple, enslave, and defeat us!

Fear is the opposite of faith. The opposite of hope. The opposite of love. The opposite of strength or power. The opposite of self-confidence.

Learning to manage, and then change our fears into faith, into confidence, is *a spiritual process* as well as a psychological and physical one.

As you learn to release your fears, you will learn to express more and more of what and whom the universe has created YOU to be: A *Divine Being*– an unlimited child of Divine Intelligence – a living, breathing *being of light, of energy*, who is temporarily walking in a human form, in a place called earth.

As you go through the *process of fear-cleansing as* discussed in this book, both in terms of learning as well as doing through provided exercises, you will find that you will have begun an *incredibly exciting and liberating journey.*

It is through this process, this journey of learning and doing, that you will be able to transform yourself energetically into the incredible spiritual being that you already inherently are, but have not yet learned to express!

As you take these actions, you will become a more efficient and effective decision-maker. You will become confident in your own decisions. You will become gentler and more sensitive to yourself and those around you in your new-found strength. You will not only be vested in who you are becoming, but you will also be *proud* of who you are transforming yourself into.

As you learn and grow you will become a better boss to those who work for you as you assist your employees become self-empowered and decisive decision-makers as they learn to become an enhanced version of themselves.

You will learn and grow to become a more effective contributor in your work space and with your colleagues.

You will become a better husband or wife.

You will become a better father or mother to your children as you learn to assist your children become the best possible version of themselves and grow up with self-confidence and an enhanced self-esteem instead of relying upon others to make decisions for them.

Finally, as you go through this process, you will be helping to liberate the planet and cleansing it of fear, assisting a new age of compassion and enlightenment to emerge.

Our objective is to learn how to manage, and remove, as many fears as possible because every single fear we remove allows our *"blanket of limitations"* to shrink and become less heavy and cumbersome. In turn, it will give us the freedom to express more and more of the goodness and abundance we already, naturally, are.

You will also discover that you will have an indescribable reservoir of "new, fresh, re-invigorated energy" at your disposal, which will ultimately create an unlimited freedom, as your fear despair energy dissipates.

In essence, you will experience a new, *spiritual energy, an energy of optimism, an energy of enthusiasm for life.*

You will replace your former fear energies with uplifting and creative thoughts that can be used to attract the things you really want in your life, but which you had come to believe *you did not deserve, or could not have.*

For example, some of you may desire to have just enough money to pay your rent this month without worry, or to have sufficient prosperity to buy both food and prescriptions, or perhaps just a little more abundance than that.

Others may desire to find a mate, or may want to have a happier and more satisfying marriage.

Other people may want better health.

Others may want a more satisfying job or career.

Still others may want to remove addictions or depression. Others may desire to clear suicidal thoughts.

In contrast, some people may want *unlimited abundance, health, AND loving relationships.*

As you clear your fears (since fear is the taproot underlying all negative limiting conditions) you will learn *you can attract* every one of these possibilities/outcomes because they are all at your beckon call.

In other words, you will learn how to make the seemingly impossible – possible!

By doing so, you now have the opportunity, to become the *Master of your own Destiny.*

Fear blocks your good. It is at the core of everything that is less than wonderful in your world: It makes no difference whether it is in your relationships, your job, your health, or your money.

As you learn to release your fears, you will find your blanket of limitations being reduced, and in this new vacuum, the universe will flood your world with Goodness, Divine Guidance, Abundance, Love, Peace, and Health.

As a result, you will find yourself living such an uplifting life that when fearful challenges come to you in the future, as they spiritually must, they will enter your world as *pebbles* and not as *boulders*. You will have the new knowledge, the new power, and the new tools to quickly identify them; and instantaneously cast them out of your world while they are still in the pebble form and are easily manageable!

Fear is the greatest single obstacle to mankind's spiritual growth and freedom!

As we learn to manage and clear the fears we have carried with us over the years, we will elevate our spiritual consciousness, and become more like God desires us to be while we live this lifetime in earth.

This is the next step in *your* personal spiritual quest - as well as mankind's.

Not only is this your spiritual quest – it is also your destiny!

As you master this process, you will learn The Secret *Keys to Freedom* and the kind of total fulfillment and personal power you can have in your existence; a life that will only be possible through the ending of fear.

You will create within you, a personal ability to be able to use and express the power Jesus discussed when he stated "You can do greater things than I have done" (2 Corinthians 5:21) and, "It is done unto you as you believe" (Mathew 8:13).

Together, "we will make the normally, impossible, possible"!

We will explore, heal, and transform the greatest fears we have carried and have woven into the blanket of limitations we have tightly wrapped around ourselves:

- A fear of feeling powerless; at the mercy of others; a fear of authority figures

- A fear of losing our job; being broke; a fear of being evicted

- A fear of losing who and what we are - our own identity

- A fear of not being loved or of not finding someone to love

- A fear of illness and disease

- A fear of being judged and criticized by others

- A fear of feeling inferior and lesser than others

- A fear of our own Death

- A fear of what happens to us after death and if we will fail to exist

A fear of being angry and hiding it beneath the surface ready to explode.

A NEW PARADIGM: RECOGNIZING YOUR COMPLETENESS

"I must not fear. Fear is the mind-killer. Fear is the little-death that brings total obliteration."

—Frank Herbert

We begin our journey to gain personal freedom by first becoming consciously aware, and then, accepting the truth through our personal demonstrations - that each of us is *complete by design, by creation.*

The famous American psychologist Abraham Maslow referred to the name of the state we are working to achieve as being *self-actualization.* He was best known for creating Maslow's Hierarchy of Needs; a theory of psychological health based on fulfilling innate human needs in priority order. Maslow identified these needs beginning with survival, then transitioning into safety, love/belonging, and esteem; and ultimately, ending in self-actualization.

He defined self-actualization as being the full use and exploitation of our being. In other words, where we take full advantage of our talents, capabilities, and potential to the highest possible degree. In other words, he believed that people are constantly in the process of striving to reach their full potential.

Maslow also believes that self-actualization is not an endpoint of a destination. It is an ongoing process in which people continue to stretch themselves and achieve new heights of well-being, creativity, and fulfillment.

Maslow went further with his definition and believed that self-actualizing people possess a number of key characteristics. Some include self-acceptance, spontaneity, independence, and the ability to have peak experiences.

I agree with Maslow's definition of self-actualization to the degree he went with his definition. However, I believe his definition of self-actualization needs to go further.

I refer to self-actualization as personal mastery, or the mastery over self. I also do not believe we can reach, or maintain a state of self-actualization unless we also include the spiritual self, who we are at our core, in addition to our human psychological state.

The reason is that we are not human beings who are attempting to become spiritual. Rather, we are spiritual beings who are temporarily living in an earth body so we can temporarily, at least for one lifetime, experience the learnings and experiences associated with the earth plane of existence.

I also take Maslow's self-actualization definition and add the word to it "unlimitedness" because I believe when we unleash our inner spirituality we can become as unlimited as we believe we can become. The only thing limiting us is ourselves and our own thoughts. Self-actualization to the human being is limited. However, to the spiritual being, self-actualization or personal mastery is totally unlimited, and is a state we are continually striving to achieve and then advance, such as all the great spiritual leaders taught, including Jesus.

This state of unlimitedness is the first metaphysical or spiritual principle we need to become aware of. It is this unique *gift* each of us has been given by our Creative Source, not by some mythical gigantic white man with a long flowing beard sitting on a throne somewhere in the sky, but by the Universe, Existence, Divine Intelligence, God, or whatever name we may choose to attach to this Creative Source.

Regardless of the name which you may be comfortable using, our Creative Force is the One who brought each of us into existence at the time of conception. Today, I personally use the name God, because, over time, I released the fear of God that I had learned from formalized religion, and have become comfortable using this name in recognition of the Divinity of all existence. It took me a while to come to this comfortability so if you feel better using a different name that is perfectly understandable.

I used to be much more scientific and preferred to stick with words like Divine Intelligence or other scientific words rather than God. Today, as I have blended more and more of my mental, emotional, and spiritual bodies together, and have come to know my Creator on a much more personal and intimate basis, I have become much more comfortable using the word God, Father, or Mother/Father/God.

During this lifetime, each one of us, regardless of the circumstances we may currently find ourselves in, have the opportunity to individually express our unique *gift of unlimitedness,* which along with life, were the most previous gifts given to us at the time of our conception.

This is our ideal, our objective, our potential, our spiritual goal. This is our aspiration. It does not mean we have currently reached this level of spirituality since it is an ongoing process. It does mean that each of us does possess this *inner unlimitedness* despite where we may presently find ourselves on Maslow's hierarchy of needs. Therefore, all we have to do is to realize it and learn to begin to express more and more of our spiritual unlimitedness. We will increasingly do this as we learn to clear our fears and limitations.

That is part of the secret. We have already been created complete, perfect, and unlimited, by design. All we have to do is to learn to believe it, clear our fears, re-focus our thoughts, and allow the universe to manifest for us in accordance with natural spiritual laws. As we do, our inner unlimitedness, our self-actualization, our personal mastery over self, will emerge and express itself.

This is the secret to how we will learn to transform ourselves and bring a state of spiritual transcendence into who and what we already are in our divine inner core.

None of us are yet complete in how we think, how we act, how we behave toward others, or even how we judge, or treat ourselves.

However, regardless of where we may presently be on our individual pathway, it does not detract from the spiritual truth that each of us *has been created complete, perfect, /unlimited – at our magnificent inner core- and that we are simply in the process of learning how to discover, and express the magnificence which God has already created us to be!*

Each of us, whether we are consciously aware of it or not, is immersed in a *process of learning, a process that is universal, unlimited, and magnificent.* It is a life's-long journey, wherein we will learn how to comprehend, and then either partially, or completely, express the gift of completeness which we have been given while living in earth this lifetime.

Earth, our temporary home of existence, has been designed as a part of this learning experience. Its purpose is to teach us many things. These include the importance of balance, of clearing fear, and of seeing beauty in everything within our field of vision which includes ourselves and others, while concurrently learning to express our unlimited spirituality despite being in a physical body.

Earth exists to give us the opportunity to spiritually grow from these types of learning opportunities. It is why we have chosen to live here during this lifetime experience.

Earth will continue to exist, despite the many challenges it faces, as long as there is a need for us to learn these types of lessons.

EXERCISE 1

How do you React to
Learning Something New?

At this time, I would like each of you to get a piece of paper or a journal. Keep it available as we go through this publication together.

As we progress, I will periodically ask you to write down the thoughts you currently have regarding questions you will be asked in various exercises such as this one. Your answers will constitute your own private and confidential spiritual journal.

I also want you to be aware that every single exercise you will be asked to do has been specifically designed to help you to grow and expand your capabilities.

The reason this is so important is that metaphysicians from Aristotle's day to today have a tendency to be overread, but underdone. There is a challenge associated with becoming highly knowledgeable if your new awareness stays intellectual and is not put into action, because it can never become wisdom, until it is used.

The knowledge you will gain on this journey, while fascinating, will not allow you to transform yourself. You can only accomplish that transformation through your own actions.

Our objective is to accomplish both. That is the reason why the exercises throughout this publication have not only been designed to help you become aware of new insights into yourself but also assist you to put that new knowledge into action. You will discover there is a huge difference between reading and doing. That is the reason you will come to appreciate the exercises!

For example, in this exercise, I would like you to answer the following questions:

1. How do you feel about learning something new?

2. How do you react emotionally and mentally when you are asked to learn something that you haven't experienced before?

3. Is it scary?

4. Does it feel threatening?

5. Or, is it exciting?

6. Is it something you look forward to doing and are pleased the opportunity has presented itself?

7. Or, is it something you attempt to avoid?

Don't worry about how your answers sound. Just write your reaction to these questions in your journal. Again, it is confidential and only you ever need to see it.

It will also be exciting for you to go back in the future and reread what you have written. When you do, you will discover how much you will have learned and grown, as you have transformed yourself.

And, I assure you, you will – as you continue on this path.

△

Your new learning and doing process will become *your new paradigm*, which I assure you will genuinely be a fundamentally different way of thinking and behaving!

Instead of believing we were born in sin and are potentially doomed to hell; the spiritual truth is that we were created in completeness by a loving, and perfect God; and that we are simply in the process of *learning* how to live and function within the reality of this spiritual truth – this new paradigm.

The question then becomes what happens after death occurs. The vast majority of religions believe that life after death is a fundamental. While the definition of life after death takes on differences between denominations it is nevertheless a common belief that some part of us such as a soul continues to exist.

More than half of the world's population believes in an ongoing existence of life and they call it reincarnation. Even in America the subject of reincarnation is becoming more commonly accepted as 33% have this belief.

While everyone has the right to choose what they believe about life after death, it is my personal belief that the beauty of the spiritual journey we are on is that we are not limited to one lifetime to learn how to fully live and experience the unlimited perfection in which we were created.

Instead, we, individually, determine how many lifetimes of learning we need and choose. In other words, *there is no time limit for our learning process, only what we choose to impose upon ourselves.* It may be one lifetime, it may be ten, or it may be hundreds. Whichever, it is our choice, and we are the decision-makers in our own destiny.

Everything is Energy

The Creative Source of the Universe, God, *is All* that exists and is all of existence. Nothing can, or does, exist outside of the Source of that Energy. God is Divine Perfection, Perfect energy, All Substance.

God created all energy into existence as an Infinite Love Thought and Source. Therefore, nothing can exist anywhere, outside of that Love, Goodness, and totally positive energy that is God.

God thought into this energy source and transformed it into substance, or material. Therefore, *everything that is of substance,* no matter what form it may take, has been molded from this same, identical, single positive energy Source of creation that came into being at the time of conception.

All substance is, and has been, created within this Love, this Perfection of Divine Goodness.

This means that the physical bodies we inhabit consist of this energy as it manifests in the form of our human body. It means that the car we drive consists of this energy which has manifested into the form of an automobile. The same is true with the chair we sit on, the business organization we work in, or any other thing that has manifested into the form or substance it now exists in.

Therefore, there is nothing can stand in opposition to this divine energy of Infinite Intelligence, except in our human or earth minds.

As our Creative Source thought into its own Energy Source, it created mankind from a Love Thought. Therefore, mankind, the human body, as a form of material substance, is also a complete Love Thought created from Divine, Perfect Energy.

Man's inner nature is completeness/total perfection/unlimitedness. It can never be anything other than this at its inner core - despite whatever negative behaviors man may exhibit.

Along with this Magnificent Gift at Origin, God also gave mankind *Free Will or Free Agency*, the opportunity to discover and *earn* his divinity, and in turn, to learn how to *create* and *express* the uniqueness of his own divinity in his every thought and action. Therefore, in his inner core, man is comprised of the same pure, positive energy of Love and Goodness as is our Divine Source.

Similar to God, as man thinks into this energy source, his thoughts manifest into substance, into material, into form. In turn, this substance becomes the things that populate the world we all live in. Material substance manifests in the form of everything that is all around us, regardless of whether that is war or peace, love or hate, disease or health, poverty or abundance. It is the *net result* of the collective thought consciousness from all mankind, influenced and combined by our own thoughts and beliefs.

Each individual, similar to our Creative Force, activates his own experiences by and through his own thoughts and beliefs. As each of us thinks into this positive energy that surrounds and permeates us, we personally create the individual world we choose to manifest as our own, the world we live in, every moment of every day.

Illustratively, if our personal life is presently filled with debt and poverty, we are using our thoughts and beliefs to create debt and poverty within our individualized world.

In contrast, if we are thinking positive thoughts about abundance, and we believe in our natural birthright to have the same unlimited prosperity as God has created (such as the unlimited number of leaves on a tree or the unimaginable number of grains of sand in a beach) we can manifest that abundance in our world.

It is our choice by right of our own consciousness which is the combination of our collective thoughts and beliefs regarding what we may or may not have in our individual world that we live in.

In other words - you will manifest in your individual world – what you believe! *Not what you hope or what you wish, but what you believe.*

This is the spiritual truth underlying the magnificent inner being that all of mankind is and that we are.

Our challenge is in learning how to use all of the energy we have been given - that surrounds and permeates us – and to do so in a positive manner, not in a destructive one. This is our challenge and our individual growth opportunity.

When we allow ourselves to become fearful, we take those positive thoughts and cause them to manifest into fearful experiences within our individualized world. In other words, we convert the positive energy at our disposal - into negative energy. Once we start this negative process, a downward cycle begins that is difficult to stop. It is similar to the death spiral we will discuss in future books with business organizations.

We use this negativity to transform our former positive energy into negative behavior, which, in turn, we use to critically judge ourselves; criticize others; gossip about other people; believe we need to judge and put others down to advance ourselves; assume we must be poor to be religiously acceptable to God; believe in ill health; believe in evil; and in limitation.

The more we engage in these behaviors, the more we lose our self-love, self-confidence, and self-esteem.

This is a quest, a timeless journey that will require numerous lifetimes to achieve - or at least as many lifetimes as we individually determine.

Personally, I have accepted that as much as I may desire to fully release and express the entire magnificent inner being this lifetime that my Creative Source has created within me, it is a high probability that I will not reach anywhere near that exalted spiritual state this lifetime.

However, despite that, it does not mean that I will not try as much as I can to move in that direction, and to *express* as *much of the magnificent nature of myself* that I already am.

This is the purpose of earth. It is also my personal goal.

It also means that the more positive movement I make toward this goal, *the easier my earth life will become.*

In other words, I am not doomed to be what I have created myself to be at the moment, with all the limitations that I may have chosen to surround myself with.

Every single limitation, every fear that I conquer and remove from my world – this lifetime - will provide me the opportunity to allow more of the Divine positive energy *to manifest into what it is that I truly desire to be in my world this lifetime, and in future lifetimes.*

Why?

Because the more we learn to heal and cleanse fear from our beliefs and thoughts, the purer our correspondence becomes with what we truly want to have in our lives now and forever. Through our new positive attracting capability, like a magnet, our cleansed being will draw back to us that which we correspond with.

In other words, what we seek will seek us in return. This is the spiritual law of the universe and it *always* works as God created it to operate.

God *never* limits us. We can only limit ourselves.

This is how God's Love Manifestation Formula works and how it expresses Itself in our individualized worlds.

It works with everything that exists regardless of whether it is with our individual lives, our families, or an organization of two or more people regardless of whether it may be business, non-profit, teachers, healthcare, government, police, or firefighters.

THE MORE FEARS YOU REMOVE – THE MORE YOU WILL RELEASE YOUR INNER MAGNIFICENCE

"Fear is only as deep as the mind allows". —Japanese Proverb

Allow me to go into further depth about the learning process in which we are engaged. During our life journeys, as individuals, we will make many mistakes, or *errors*, since we are not yet perfect in our expressions while we are in earth. Those mistakes or errors are simply a part of our learning process, or journey, since we have requested the opportunity to *earn the perfection* we were given at creation.

One of the fundamental things we need to learn about our lifelong path of learning is that there is *no reason, no purpose or positive advantage in judging or criticizing ourselves for making errors*, despite what earth has tried to teach us.

Earth also attempts to teach us that we must be *punished* when we make an error. That also is not true.

Instead, with the new knowledge we will acquire, we will come to learn that there are positive benefits from the errors we make. That and *that alon*e is their only purpose. After making an error, we can learn how to do better the next time - when the opportunity presents itself in the future – which it always will do.

This is similar to our junior high school experience in a spelling class. When we made a spelling mistake, an error, it did not mean we were a bad person and needed to be punished. It did not mean we had to criticize or negatively judge ourselves. It did not mean we had to stand in front of the class and be ridiculed. All it meant was that we simply needed to learn how to spell the word correctly the next time. Nothing more, nothing less!

Similarly, our Creative Source knows that we will make errors on our journey as we explore and learn more about our Divine Nature. This is simply a part of our learning process to *achieve* and *earn* our Divine Completeness.

It is also why God gave us a pencil at the beginning of our journey with a big eraser at the end so when we do make errors, which we will inevitably do in our quest to fully discover our spiritual selves, we simply need to look at the error, learn from it, erase it, forgive ourselves; move on; and hopefully don't repeat the same mistake again.

It is not a *sin* to make an error. The word *Sin* was an old archery term that *simply meant to* "miss the mark with an arrow". Nothing more, nothing less.

It was man, not God, who decided that *sin*, when "interpreted" according to man's biases, could become an incredibly powerful tool to control our belief systems. As a result, religion created specific rules and religious dogma, beneficial to themselves, and then wrapped such fearful concepts as guilt, judgment day, and hell around the word *sin*. In doing so, they converted the process of simply making an error and learning from it, into one of the most fearful concepts ever devised by man.

Making an error, or simply missing the mark, should not in any way be associated with fear, guilt, punishment, limitation, or potential banishment to hell.

It is why we do not surround our children with punishment or guilt when they try something for the first time and make an error while doing so. Otherwise, our children would be perpetually hell-bound when they fall while learning to walk; misspell a word; take a spill from a bicycle; or answer a question incorrectly.

God never created fear. Fear was created by man, in earth!

This understanding is crucial, because it brings to our conscious awareness the knowledge regarding how the earth has attempted to convince us that fear is real.

When we dissect and examine fear and its associated false concepts, we will recognize how fear has been used to control our beliefs, and in turn, limit how we think and function. This new knowledge will allow us to return to our roots of spiritual freedom as we begin our process to remove it.

Earth is but one place of learning among many for us on our journey to spiritual freedom so we can ultimately become fully complete and unlimited. It is a place where we have enormous opportunities to express what we believe our spiritual inner nature to be so we can learn from those experiences, both the positive outcomes as well as the errors we will make.

Earth is a fantastic teacher, and is one of the many places we will experience in our journey to achieve completeness with our Creative Source. Each place of learning will provide specific lessons we need to learn. The reason that earth is such a phenomenal teacher is that earth believes in the concept of fear. In turn, it teaches us about the insidious power fear can have in controlling and limiting how we think and function mentally and emotionally. It uses religion, government, business, and societal norms to ground us in fearful beliefs, and then reinforces those beliefs over and over and over again until we accept earth's truths as being *our truths*.

However, once we learn our lesson regarding the falsity of fear, we will no longer have the need to accept fear into our lives. We can banish it, forever, into the nothingness from which it has come since it has no origin in God. It is only an illusion of earth.

In other words, since God did not create Fear – it can only exist in our own thoughts and minds – and only for as long as we choose to accept and believe in it. Once we learn this lesson we can graduate from all fear and limitation. We will no longer need to accept anything other than positive things in our world as we learn more and more about our own unlimited completeness.

The purpose of this book is to help us to remember, to learn, that fear is simply an artificial earth concept that has become real in our world – only because we have allowed it to do so. This awareness, and our use of this new knowledge, will give us the ability to begin the process of releasing fear's hold on us as we reduce the blanket of fear and limitations we have created and wrapped around ourselves.

As you do this, you will discover that each of us personally possesses greater power and strength than you have ever known to be possible.

The more fear and limitations you remove - the more you will positively release and manifest what you desire in your world.

Conversely, the more fear and limitations you keep stored within, the less energy you will have to create the positive things you want in your life!

At conception, we were born with an inner being of spiritual perfection and completeness. We wrapped a physical body around it so we could walk in earth, among the fears of earth, and determine how we wanted to react in response to the fears of earth.

This is similar to the body suit the diver uses when they are going to explore great depths of the ocean or that the astronauts wear when they are going to outer space.

We had a choice. Our choice was to choose love or fear, good or evil, abundance or poverty, loving companionship or loneliness, health or illness. When we attempted to choose both, *duality,* we created internal conflict and began the process of believing we were *separate* from our God Source.

The truth is *we can never separate* ourselves from our Creative Source because that would be impossible. Nevertheless, we can temporarily believe it to be possible.

The Divine Energy within which we were created is complete and positive energy. It cannot contain anything of a negative nature. However, we, in our own minds, have the ability to convert that positive energy into a negative-based energy source which can then manifest into such episodes or experiences as fear, anger, hate, violence, poverty, loneliness, and illness.

This is one of the major differences between God and each one of us.

God does not, and cannot, cause negative things

The only one that can do so is us, individually, and collectively; and mankind as a whole.

In other words, individually, and collectively, *we are the only ones* who can convert the all-positive divine energy at our disposal (which God bestowed upon each of us at conception) and convert it into destructive behavior and outcomes.

This includes our making choices between having poverty or abundance, love or hate, fear or self-confidence, illness or health, peace or war, in our individualized world.

Or, we can convert that same energy into only positive energy, thoughts and behaviors; and in turn, *transcend ourselves; and experience a divine spiritual shift.*

It is the personal choice our Creative Source has given each of us - the right to choose! We can also call it *Free Will*.

So, I suggest you choose wisely my friend. The rest of your life depends on it.

WE TEMPORARILY WALK ON EARTH WITH A HUMAN BODY

"Fear is the path to the Dark Side. Fears lead to anger, anger leads to hate, hate leads to suffering"

—Ruth Gendlen

Many, at first, have difficulty believing, or accepting, that God is an energy source; or that each of us at our core is an energy being; and that we possess a magnificent inner being that is complete/unlimited/perfect – even though our inner perfection was created by an All-Loving God of Completeness.

This is why I suggest it is valuable to go back and re-watch *Cocoon*, the 1985 movie classic.

As a God-light energy source, we are comparable in many ways to the aliens in that movie. Directed by Oscar award winner Ron Howard, the film earned academy awards for Best Supporting Actor and Best Visual Effects. Starring Don Ameche, Brian Dennehy, and Wilford Brimley, the movie is a fantasy in which the residents of a Florida rest home get a new lease on life when they stumble across an alien "fountain of youth" in a disused holiday home. Unbeknown to them, aliens have been using the swimming pool in the house to store their cocooned brethren, giving the waters in the indoor swimming pool a powerful, rejuvenating energetic quality, which the retired residents from the rest home use to rejuvenate themselves. The aliens are actually benevolent energy source beings who have temporarily wrapped themselves within a human body so they can survive the earth experience.

While a fantasy, it is amazing how accurate the film is in terms of each of us being energy sources who have chosen to temporarily wrap a human body around ourselves so we can experience the earth episode, the life we are in the midst of living.

It is well worth our while to review this film again and again, along with its sequel, Cocoon, The Return; in order to articulate and reinforce in our own minds the new knowledge we are gaining in regard to the spiritual reality of who and what we are – energy beings of completeness.

Part of the learning process on our way to realizing our completeness is to identify, examine, and come face to face with our individual fears so we can learn how to clear them from our consciousness. The more we do this, the more we allow our inner magnificence to manifest and make our walk-in earth this lifetime - easier than it had been previously.

The more fears you harbor, the more challenging and difficult your life becomes. The more fears you clear from your consciousness the better you allow divine love and goodness to flood in and replace the fear that used to occupy that space.

We know that nature abhors a vacuum. This is what is meant by that statement.

The goal of the earth is to grow spiritually. How you do it is up to you to decide. Personally, I find that as long as I have the opportunity to choose how I want to spiritually grow, then I would prefer to do it with as full and abundant a life experience as possible, and conversely one with as few major problems as possible. While I know that problems are necessary for change to occur, I personally prefer to deal with what I call challenges because that keeps them in the energy state of a pebble, rather than allowing them to grow into the form of a boulder.

The beauty of the learning universe we live in is that every single one of us gets to make that personal decision. Since we are a unique and individual aspect of our Creative Source, we have each been given the opportunity to choose what it is we want to experience for ourselves.

We *cannot achieve our full completeness if we have both love and fear mixed within our consciousness.* The reason is that *fear is from earth and is temporary.* Love is from the spiritual realm and is *permanent.*

But it goes much further than even that. The reason we cannot have both fear and faith is that they are polar opposites. To practice faith is to live without being controlled by fear. Having *faith* means having the courage to operate in faith knowing that - even though our good has not yet manifested in a physical form - we BELIEVE and KNOW that it will!

It is also the primary purpose of this book: To transform our fear into Faith, so we may release and become the magnificent beings we already are!

However, please note that I am not expecting you to have *blind faith*. That would defy your logic, your intellect, and mine. And, that is not how the universe works. Instead, we will provide you with new knowledge and spiritual principles throughout this publication.

Then, through the exercises, and your own use of the new knowledge you will be acquiring, you will discover that these principles actually work, for you! That will be the time when this knowledge will cease to be academic or philosophical.

At that time, it will become real for you, because you will have found it to be true in your world. That will be the time when your new knowledge will become faith, because it will have been transformed into your personal belief system.

When we are living in and expressing nothing but our positive energy – we are *unlimited*. We are capable of achieving anything. Nothing is impossible.

The impossible becomes possible - for us!

In contrast, the more we learn to integrate fear into our consciousness, the more we learn to limit ourselves and become less than complete. The more fear we absorb into our existing positive energy, the more we convert ourselves from being immersed within a positive "can do energy" into becoming more negative in our thoughts and behaviors.

It is a Spiritual Law: Like attracts Like. The more fears we accumulate, the more fears we will continue to attract and create in the future.

The more prominent our negative vibration, the more that negative energy will impact the way we think and behave on a daily basis. It will drive us in a downward cycle that, like a magnet, will attract everything to itself of a negative nature. This includes a lack of self-confidence, loneliness, poverty, disease, mental illness, depression, and suicide.

We know from modern science that energy cannot be lost or destroyed, it can only be transformed. Therefore, we know that as a life force of energy created by our Creative Force, we cannot ever cease to exist. However, we can, and do, *continually change form and substance through our learning experiences.*

Today, for example, we look totally different than the way we looked when we were a baby, or when we became an infant, or a teenager, or middle-aged. Yet, inside, we maintain the same "perpetual self" or "unique personality", or psyche that we were while all those changes in form were taking place.

We have wrapped a physical body around ourselves to learn the lessons of earth. That is all.

At the end of our earthly life, when we experience an earth death, we do not cease to exist. We simply again change form/substance at the time of death, discard the human body we wore for this earth life, and then continue forward with our life's journey. Again, very similar to our transition from a baby to an infant, to a teenager, to middle-age, to elderly.

However, despite changing form, we always maintain our personality, our soul, our persona, the thing that makes each one of us uniquely *"who we are"*. This cycle of learning is continuous until we *earn* the total completeness with our God Source that we were initially created to be.

The difference is that each of us will then have *earned* the gift that we were initially *given* at creation. This is the *Sense of Purpose* we were given at conception: To earn our completeness.

As a part of this process, we will bring lessons we had not completely worked out in previous earth lives into our current life until we resolve them with our new knowledge. For example, if we experienced different kinds of fear episodes that we had not cleared from previous lives, those experiences will become learning lessons we will have an opportunity to resolve in this earth life or in future earth lives when we have earned sufficient strengths to do so.

Earth is but one place for learning. We will continue to experience different lifetimes here in earth, each with its unique lessons of learning, until we gain the knowledge to clear fear and its insidious control over our beliefs and thought patterns. Then we will be free from fear and will graduate from the earth experience.

In this manner, each of us is in a continuous, life-cycle process to not only learn, but also to *earn* the divinity, the perfection, the unlimitedness, that God created each of us to be in the beginning.

We will carry out this process in many places of learning, earth being but one of the many.

WE BEGIN THIS LIFE WITH LESSONS FROM PRIOR LIVES

"A physical injury immobilizes a person, whereas psychological trauma incapacitates by inflicting fear, taking away an individual's desire to live."

—Vince Flynn

Like all of us, I came into this life with unresolved spiritual lessons from previous lives, coupled with the many strengths which I had developed during those same lifetimes. This was done for the spiritual objective of continuing to clear the fears I had previously started to work on - but had not yet completely healed. Mine included a fear of authority figures, a feeling of inadequacy based on a lack of self-confidence in my own abilities, a fear of God, and a fear of abundance. Once back in earth's fear vibration I also added new fears entirely on my own.

While between lives, each of us creates an *inventory* of the strengths we gained from our previous lives, along with the limitations/fears we acquired during those lifetimes. We develop this inventory together with our spiritual mentors and teachers who are able to see with a larger vision than we possess at that moment. They have graduated from the earth experience so they can see from a helicopter view in contrast to the limited earth vision we possess at that moment.

This inventory analysis is as close as we will ever come to what has been referred to as Judgment Day by formalized religion whereby Saint Peter and God supposedly stand by the Pearly Gates and determine who does and does not get into heaven by studying the ledger sheet of sins they have tallied against each person requesting admission.

In contrast, the inventory process we are referring to is NOT judgmental in any way, shape, or form.

Instead, it is simply a learning review of what we did well and did not do well during our previous incarnation together with an analysis of the strengths and fears we have accumulated during prior lives. From this inventory we determine the fears we choose to conquer in our next lifetime together with the strengths we choose to bring with us to achieve that objective. It is as simple or as profound as that.

It includes the many fears we had previously healed during our spiritual journeys to earth, as well as those yet to be fully healed. It also contains the numerous strengths we accumulated and would need to use in this lifetime to conquer our remaining fears/limitations because when we return to earth, *we always do so with more strengths than we will ever need to conquer the fear limitations we are coming to heal.*

This process evolves into choosing the parents, relatives, friends, and circumstances into which we chose to be born this lifetime. This is the reason why family units tend to stay together although in different roles in future lifetimes.

Our birth was not random or accidental. Nor were the earth conditions we surrounded ourselves with at birth. Instead, our parents and surrounding earth circumstances were *macro-designed by each of us, you and me, while we were beyond earth,* to provide us with optimum learning opportunities so we could continue to advance our spiritual growth during this earth lifetime.

In other words, between lives, *we* choose the learning environment in which we can most effectively continue to learn and grow *–this lifetime.*

Obviously, we are not consciously aware of this while we are in the earth plane because if we were, the earth would no longer continue to be a place of spiritual growth and learning for us. It would cease to exist because it would have lost its purpose. It would simply become the illusion that it really is, but which we have not yet grown to understand or accept.

The most important aspect of this knowledge to be aware of is that *we have been involved* in creating the circumstances into which we were born this lifetime. Our birth, parents, relatives, friends, and circumstances including nationality, race, sex, abundance, debt, illness, health, love, or loneliness, did not happen by accident or circumstance.

Recently, there has been a great deal of publicity and confusion about sexuality including heterosexual, homosexual, lesbian, bisexual, pansexual, transgender, and LGBTQ. I have been frequently asked about this. My answer is that at the time of our divine conception we were each created male or female. That is the sexual orientation we are most comfortable with and it will be the predominant orientation we take into future lives.

For example, I was conceived as a male and am most comfortable being a heterosexual male. However, in order to experience different lessons associated with sexuality, we will periodically be born into an earth body with the opposite sex for learning purposes. When this happens, it is natural that that person may feel somewhat uncomfortable with their new sexuality until they become accustomed to it. The initial awkwardness may be because they likely don't understand why they are feeling the way they are without this understanding.

In other instances, in a past life, we may have developed a hatred or hostility toward a person who was a homosexual or lesbian and it was this fear vibration that prompted us to return to this lifetime with that sexual orientation so we could clear and heal our fear. Remember, what you fear or what you love will always be attracted to you because that is the spiritual law of the universe.

It is also natural, normal, and common for young people to be confused or question their sexuality. This occurs because essentially, they are in the process of *questioning everything about themselves* as they transition from an infant into an adult body. It is not sex alone they question, although society is attempting to make this the predominant thought and issue at the moment.

Finally, sometimes a person who is normally male returns to earth quicker than the normal return cycle while having selected a different sex for the body they have chosen. When that happens, it can lead to some additional sexual orientation confusion until they become comfortable with who and what they are.

Society has had different sexual orientations for thousands of years. It is not just today. For example, in some societies, homosexuality was considered perfectly natural and was even viewed by some as being superior. Again, like everything, sexuality provides learning opportunities. It is not right or wrong. It is just another learning experience provided by the earth plane of consciousness.

Again, the entire macro-level of our future life in earth, our birth, parents, sex, wealth or poverty, love or violence, was *spiritually planned by each of us in conjunction with our spiritual mentors.*

Another question I am frequently asked is whether that means everything is *predestined* or *preordained*? It is not.

We, in conjunction with our spiritual teachers and mentors, determine the macro-level design of our next life so we can experience optimal opportunities to identify and clear our fears while progressing to our spiritual unlimitedness. But that is where it ends. At that point, once we enter the earth plane, our Free Will, which we were also given at the time of divine conception, provides us the opportunity to determine how we choose to work with the circumstances we created for ourselves while we are in the earth vibration.

In other words, everything has not been pre-ordained or destined. This is the reason we are walking on earth in a learning mode. We each have the opportunity to choose, through our own Free Will, what it is we want to choose, and what we decide to do with the circumstances we have placed ourselves into for learning purposes.

This new knowledge also means we can no longer claim we are a VICTIM of our birth circumstances and therefore have no choice but to accept the conditions we were born into.

The truth is – *None of us are victims* – and none of us need to accept the circumstances in which we may find ourselves, regardless of how dire they may momentarily appear to be. Our purpose is to change those conditions as we deem necessary to grow spiritually!

As an example, I thought it might be helpful to share the circumstances I chose to be born into and why those decisions were made from a spiritual, *beyond earth,* perspective. Like many of us, I chose to be born into a dysfunctional family. Not dysfunctional to the degree that there was physical violence or abuse. Just the opposite. My mother was a stay-at-home mom who ran the household and managed the finances for the family while my dad worked and made the income. My mother adored me as her firstborn. I could do no wrong in her eyes - no matter what I did. I was *perfect* in her eyes, as she viewed perfection – even though I knew I was far from perfect – which created conflicts in my self-confidence.

She also loved me to the point that she was overly protective. Without meaning to do so, she taught me that I always needed to seek her guidance before I made a decision. On the surface, this appeared to be a good thing. In actuality, it helped to reinforce a lack of belief in my own abilities which I had previously created through fear in prior lives.

My father was the opposite of my mother in many ways. He was multi-talented in numerous disciplines, but was quiet to the point of being shy and nearly introverted, particularly in the early part of his life. He worked for the post office and gradually ascended the ranks from a letter sorter to becoming assistant post master. We were financially in the lower to medium middle class while I was growing up.

My Dad was a workaholic and I learned from him that you had to work hard to survive. We never went hungry but money was tight and decisions were always economically considered. Like most fathers at the time, he hid his emotions, was never emotionally demonstrative, and never verbally let me know he loved me until shortly before his death.

My father expressed his love for me through work. He got me my first part-time job when I was ten years old to teach me the importance of money and that you had to work hard to make money. Later, as an adult, he would fix things in my home such as plumbing or electrical concerns without ever saying a word. That was his form of expressing love.

Neither my mother nor father had gone to college so there was no encouragement for me to attend college. The learning that I *was not college material* came from my high school home room teacher.

He had once run an experiment in class asking every student what they planned to do after graduation. Not knowing what I wanted to do, I expressed as a few others had done, and stated that I guess I planned to go to college. My homeroom teacher stopped, *chuckled*, and then adamantly stated, "*Dick, you* need to rethink your future then because you are not smart enough to go to college!"

I was shocked and embarrassed, and would have accepted his assertion and complied since I didn't know different, if it weren't for a partial athletic scholarship, I had been offered by the church I attended. Since several of my friends were going to college, I figured I might as well go, have fun, and party a lot since based on my teacher's affirmation I now knew that I was going to flunk out anyway.

It was in this manner that a fear of authority figures, coupled with a lack of self-confidence, and the belief that money was hard to come by and could only be earned through hard work were deeply rooted in my upbringing *this lifetime.*

While I regularly attended a Lutheran church, I also frequently went to church with my friends who were Catholic, Methodist, and Jewish. This meant that I became acquainted with religious practices in addition to those from the Lutheran Church. Discussions with my friends established my childhood beliefs that God was a judgmental punishing being, one I learned to fear, who did not appreciate wealth or abundance, since the clergy leadership kept talking about how difficult it was for rich people to get into heaven. They stressed that it was much better to have just enough money to get by, even though it meant struggles – because God loves those who struggle and *bear their crosses in silence and humility.* God will then reward them - later - in heaven.

Such assertions served to create and reinforce my beliefs in limitation and lack of abundance, along with my fear of, and lack of being comfortable with God.

Despite me *expecting to flunk out of college*, a professor decided he liked my debate skills and helped me get sufficient grades so I could stay on his competitive debate team. Nevertheless, to stay on the safe side, I also became friends with some elite athletes and took advantage of the test answers they were given to ensure I passed challenging classes. Those experiences added a "fear of getting caught" to my fear inventory, together with the already existing self-confidence issues.

In this manner, *in what appears to be a normal natural pattern or flow*, the beyond-earth fear lessons I needed to work on during this lifetime manifested themselves, *like magic*, during this lifetime.

This is how the universal learning process works, and how perfect it is for all of us. We attract to ourselves the strengths and fears we chose to work on and heal before we came to earth.

We then manifest them naturally during this lifetime so they are present when we need to work on them.

Amazingly, I graduated from college, was accepted into graduate school, and got married. This provided me an opportunity to be a new husband who had to get sufficient grades to graduate while experiencing what it was like to have literally *no money to live on* while I finished the last semester of my master's degree.

We lived in a small, walk-up non-air-conditioned brick apartment in 90+ degree heat. To survive, we drove to my parent's home about 35 miles away on the weekends to share their food while taking enough from their garden to last us through the next weekend. This experience wonderfully reinforced my fear of abundance and belief in scarcity.

We later divorced, and I discovered the fears associated with my apparent inadequacy as a husband while wondering if I would ever find love again, or whether I was destined to live a life of loneliness.

In contrast, along with these earth fears/limitations, I also brought into this life experience such strengths as being a hard worker with a pleasing personality. I was very good at public speaking, was nice looking, articulate, could easily socialize with others, and could see goodness in others even though I had challenges seeing it in myself. I had also brought along with me intelligence, and a determination to succeed despite the circumstances, along with an ability to see things from both a short and long-term perspective. However, those strengths would not emerge until later in my life.

I gained an initial understanding of metaphysics from my aunt who was a practicing Rosicrucian (a 4,000-year-old, highly spiritual, secret society that had its origins in ancient Egypt). That experience occurred because my mother was early into her third pregnancy, had been told by two doctors that she could never carry to term, and would abort the child.

In contrast, my aunt confidently told my mother that she *would* deliver a healthy baby girl to full-term despite the doctors adamantly stating that she would end up aborting the child.

My aunt was known, and accepted in our family, as *being a unique and highly spiritual person, who was also a loving and fantastic healer.*

She came to live with us and performed daily healings on my mother for about 5 months.

My aunt was correct while the medical doctors were incorrect as my mom carried my sister, a healthy baby girl, to term. In turn, I began to learn the power of faith, healing, and metaphysics. My aunt also taught me that I was a good person, and needed to believe in myself.

I adored my aunt even though that knowledge about myself took me many years to accept.

These are examples of the types of experiences that I chose to bring to earth. In other words, like everyone else does, I had certainly chosen to bring many challenges (limitations/fears) into this lifetime that I needed to overcome and heal; but I had also brought many more strengths than limitations in my arsenal to do so.

There is a powerful Spiritual Law that states: You always have more strength than you need to conquer your fears and limitations!

All of us enter this earth plane with these types of fears, and strengths, all of *which are custom-designed, individually*, for each one of us, based on our prior learning experiences.

When you examine your own parentage, your upbringing, your siblings, your relatives, your friends (which we will do in the next chapter) you will discover that each *base fear* you have accumulated, regardless of whether it may be a belief in poverty, in illness, or in loneliness, has manifested itself in this lifetime so you will be able to heal them through the strengths you have also brought into this lifetime.

This is the only purpose of you attracting those fears – so you can heal them –this lifetime!

IDENTIFYING FEARS AND STRENGTHS FROM PRIOR LIVES

"We can easily forgive a child who is afraid of the dark; the real tragedy of life is when men are afraid of the light."

—Plato

I would now like you to build upon these insights and begin some very important exercises which have been designed to help you learn more about yourself, your fears, your strengths, and how others have influenced you in this lifetime. Pull out your paper or spiritual journal. Sit in a quiet place and prepare to begin writing.

The words you write will be of great assistance in helping you to identify and clear your fears so you can begin to release your magnificent inner power and achieve the good you want in your world. Remember, your words are confidential and will only be seen by you. So, I advise you to be as honest with yourself as you possibly can be.

We begin by identifying *Key Influencers* you associated with before you graduated from high school. These are individuals you grew up with who *influenced* you to think and behave in certain ways. They may have been parents, relatives, teachers, clergy members, or others.

Write their names on the left side of your page similar to what is shown below under Exercise 2. Then, next to that individual, write out in as much detail as you can remember, how they influenced you. What did you learn from them? What beliefs did they teach you when you were growing up? Was their influence on you positive or negative? If positive, how? If negative, how?

Examples of influencers in my personal life would be my parents, my aunt, my homeroom teacher, the lady who I worked for as a ten-year-old (who was a retired psychiatrist and judge), and my minister. There were many more, but those at a minimum, are influencers whom I would have to include in my life based on the experiences I previously shared about my upbringing.

It is also important that you be aware that it is extremely unlikely that everyone who influenced or impacted your life did so in a positive manner. Illustratively, you may have had an influencer in your world who was an alcoholic, and through their dysfunctional behavior, helped you develop a belief that you would *never, ever,* touch a drop of alcohol when you grew up. Or, their behavior may have impacted you to the point where you couldn't wait to start drinking since it looked like alcohol tasted so good to them.

Be as honest with yourself as possible when you are putting this information on paper. List as many of these influencers asyou can think of. Use all of the words you can think of to describe the beliefs and thoughts you acquired, and from whom they came. Use what I previously wrote about my parents, aunt, and teacher as a guide if it helps you in creating your own inventory because that is why I shared them with you

Most importantly, don't judge yourself or others while you are doing this exercise or the following two exercises. The reason is that earth is messy and has many, many, different lessons to teach. Also remember, beyond earth, it was YOU WHO CHOSE to be born into this family unit, along with the influencers you asked to become part of your world this lifetime.

Supporting the need to not judge, John Bradshaw, a family-symptoms therapy advocate and family dynamics expert, cites research that found 96% of all families to be to some degree "dysfunctional". Nearly 700,000 children are abused or neglected in the U.S. every year. Children Protective Services in the U.S. finds a sexual abuse case with minors every 9 minutes. Almost 21 million Americans have an addiction problem with alcohol, drugs, or both. 26% of Americans ages 18 and older suffer from a diagnosable mental disorder in a given year.

Based on statistics such as these, it would be surprising if you chose to be born into a perfectly functioning family unit that did not have challenges. I suggest you keep this in mind as you are writing the words on your pages.

EXERCISE 2

Your List of Influencers

My Key Influencers	Describe How You Were influenced
Mother	
Father	
Siblings	
Relatives	
Clergy	
Teachers	
Coaches	

Other Influencers

△

When you have completed this exercise, I would next like you to list the *Circumstances* you were born into which contributed to the creation of the fears you brought with you from your prior lives.

△

EXERCISE 3

Your Earth Circumstances – Your Fears and Limitations

This exercise has been designed to help you look deeper into and describe the circumstances you chose to be born into. I would like you to describe the earth conditions you chose this lifetime so the fears you brought from prior lives could manifest and allow you to heal them.

I suggest you use the following questions in writing your answers in the spiritual journal you have started. Then add anything else important to you. Remember, everything you write is confidential and need only be seen by you.

- **Question:** Were you born into poverty, or wealth: Did you have barely enough money to survive, or did you have medium wealth, or abundance?

- **Question:** Were you grappling as a family to have enough to eat and a place to live; or in contrast, were you concerned about how you could spend all the money your parents were giving you?

- **Question:** Where did your belief in abundance or poverty come from?

- **Question:** Do you believe in and feel you are entitled to prosperity and abundance? If so, how and where did this belief come from?

- **Question:** Did your parents love you, detest you, or ignore you?

- **Question:** Were either of your parents or family members addicts? Workaholics? Alcoholics? Drug abusers? How did this affect you?

- **Question:** Were either of your parents, relatives, or other influencers verbally or physically abusive? How?

- **Question:** Were either of your parents supportive of you, your dreams, your aspirations? Did they try to encourage you to dream, or did they attempt to keep you grounded in earth reality? Did they discourage your dreams? How did they do this?

- **Question:** Were you born healthy or into sickness?

- **Question:** Were either of your parents, close relatives, or friends ill? How did this affect you and your family?

- **Question:** Are you prone to good health or ill health? Why?

- **Question:** Do you believe in and feel you are entitled to good health? If so, how and where did this belief come from?

- **Question:** Are you dependent on others? Are you self-confident? Do you need others to affirm that you are okay? If so, how and where did you learn this trait?

- **Question:** Do you believe you are intelligent? If so, where did you learn this? Why do you believe it?

- **Question:** Are you self-confident in your own abilities? If so, where did this belief come from? Why do you feel this way about yourself?

- What have you learned from your church or your clergy member(s)?

- What key beliefs did your church or religion teach you that you have accepted? How did you learn this belief(s)? What did you learn from them when you were growing up?

- What other fears or limitations do you hold today? Where did they come from?

△

EXERCISE 4

Your Earth Circumstances – Your Strengths and Assets

I would now like you to transition into Exercise 4. This exercise will ask you to list the many strengths you believe you possess. The purpose is not to be humble or self-serving. It is to use these pages to identify on paper many of the assets and strengths that you believe you came to possess by the approximate time that you graduated from high school.

The processes we are using in these three exercises are comparable in some ways, although very simplistically, to the inventory you conducted with your spiritual mentors beyond earth where you identified the fears you wanted to manifest this lifetime, along with the strengths you determined you needed to heal them.

This exercise is also the beginning of a self-diagnosis of your strengths as you view them. The previous exercise was the beginning of a self-diagnosis of the fears and limitations you believe you have.

Also remember, that you came to earth with more strengths than you would ever need to conquer and heal all your fears and limitations. Don't be humble in listing them as you see and understand them today. List all that you can think of regardless of whether you are not yet certain how much of a strength they may be.

I can also assure you that you will add to your list of strengths in the future as you continue on this pathway because many of the strengths you already possess you have buried so deep beneath the fears you have created that you are likely not yet even aware of them.

These are exercises that we seldom, if ever, allow ourselves the luxury of doing while we are here on earth. Instead, we tend to just forge ahead with life without thinking much about it.

As a result, these exercises are designed to force you to identify and examine the strengths and fears you currently possess, as well as how and why you chose to bring those particular attributes with you into your learning experience this lifetime. Within this perspective, please answer the following questions in your spiritual journal:

- **Question:** Do you believe you are an important and good person? Where did this belief come from? Was it because you were born into a home where your parents believed you to be precious and treated you this way?

- **Question:** Do you have self-confidence and a belief in yourself? If so, where did this belief come from?

- **Question:** Do you believe in abundance and prosperity? Do you believe that it is fine to have abundance and that God loves prosperity?

- **Question:** Do you believe you have to work hard to gain and hold onto prosperity, especially in the form of money? Do you believe you can have prosperity this lifetime?

- **Question:** How strongly do you hold a belief in your own abilities? Do you believe you can achieve anything you set your mind to achieve?

- **Question:** Are you healthy? Were your born healthy? Has your body generally always been healthy?

- **Question:** Do you believe you deserve to be healthy and clear of any major illnesses or diseases?

- **Question:** Do you believe you are attractive or handsome?

- **Question:** Do you believe in physical and mental healings? Do you believe you have the ability to keep yourself healthy?

- **Question:** Do you believe you are intelligent and deserving of good things to happen to you? If so, why do you believe this?

- **Question:** Are you dependent on others or yourself? Do you need others to affirm that you are okay?

- **Question:** Are you a good writer or speaker?

- **Question:** Are you self-confident? Do you believe in your own abilities? Where did this belief in yourself come from?

- **Question:** What are your spiritual or religious beliefs? Do they give you spiritual freedom or a belief in limitation?

- Do you believe you are deserving of happiness, being in love, and loving someone?

- **Question:** What other strengths do you possess this lifetime?

$$\triangle$$

These beginning exercises are very important in helping you to become aware of the fears you have created and need to clear from your consciousness; as well as in identifying the many strengths you have brought into this lifetime with you.

Keep working on creating this inventory. It is not a one-time, sit-down process. Take your time. Keep adding to it over time. As you do, your conscious mind will keep being filled with other things you will want to add to your list.

Become sensitive to and aware of the fears and limitations you have exposed yourself to during the first approximate 20 years of your life, as well as all of the strengths you brought with you to eliminate those fears from your world forever.

Look again at your parents, your siblings, your other influencers, and the kind of world you grew up in. How were you influenced to accept the beliefs that you still hold today?

Most importantly, remember - You are not bound to accept the circumstances or fears you chose to be born into this lifetime. You are the only one who can choose to accept them, or overcome them if you feel they are no longer beneficial. It is your choice, and only your choice to make, since no one else can make that decision for you.

The truth is this: The more fear you choose to clear this lifetime - the more of your strengths, your own inner magnificence you will manifest–in *this lifetime that you are living.*

You will discover that as you clear your fear, more and more of your strengths will appear, as if by magic. You will discover that you have strengths you never envisioned you ever had. You are on a magical journal to discover the true reality of all that you are.

I know this on a personal basis, because it happened to me. It will also happen to you if you choose to walk this pathway of discovering the divinity of who you already are.

You are the only one who can decide when you choose to do this - and how quickly - you choose to do it!

As we close this chapter, remember: *You are not a victim.* You chose to create this life and the circumstances into which you were born, no matter how positive or dire, in order to give you your next set of earth experiences to overcome and heal on your pathway to discovering and releasing the magnificent inner being of completion already within you.

Your inner magnificence is waiting, like the beautiful butterfly, or the magnificent statue of David ready to be released from its cocoon of fear.

All that is needed is for you to begin the process of chipping away at it – identifying and healing your fears – so you can release your all- powerful and loving inner being.

Our goal in writing this book is to help you learn how to release your inner magnificence, so like the beautiful butterfly that emerged from the entrapping cocoon, you can fly above the problems of earth while reaching out your hand to help others who are also in need of finding their own inner being.

Just like you were before you picked up this publication!

YOU HAVE CONTINUED TO GROW YOUR FEARS AND YOUR STRENGTHS WHILE YOU HAVE BEEN HERE ON EARTH

"If your thoughts are filled with fear of the past, or worries about the future, it is certain that you cannot be in touch with what is deep inside you. Thus, you are not acting according to your real needs. It is fear that decides for you".

—Anoir Ou-Chad

For most of us, adulthood (the time of independence from our parents) happens around the age of 20. If we graduate from high school and do not choose to go to college, adulthood arrives at the time of our first full-time job, or when we join the military services. For those who choose to attend college, their first full-time job is delayed until they are in their early twenties.

The majority who are reading this publication are independent of their parents. However, despite being adults, we tend to keep the core influences (beliefs, fears, and strengths) we accumulated during childhood.

Those childhood thought patterns remain dominant in our current thought patterns as adults, especially the fears and beliefs in limitations. Earth believes in fear and continually reinforces it in numerous ways including societal norms.

The core beliefs we accepted during our formative years have also continued to grow and expand. That is, unless we have dramatically changed ourselves in between, which is highly unlikely. Accordingly, the probability is extremely high that each of us has continued to expand the original fears we brought to earth, while concurrently continuing to grow our belief in limitation, both in thought as well as in material form.

Most of us, as we become an adult, do not magically shut off a switch that stops us from continuing to be ruled by the fears and limitations we accepted in our youth. In contrast, those limiting thoughts tend to grow and expand despite our becoming much more adept as adults in trying to camouflage them, so "supposedly" others *will not be able to see our flaws.*

As we continue the journey to release our inner magnificence, it is necessary *to build upon* the previous exercises we just completed, so we can gain a more complete inventory of the fears and limitations, as well as the strengths we have *added to and expanded* since our youth.

Remember, we always have more strengths than needed to overcome the fears we have created. So, we also need to reflect all of those factors in our inventories for them to be up-to-date and realistic.

As in the last chapter, I will use myself as an example. I married while in college. A few years later the marriage ended in divorce. I know I contributed mightily to the divorce. I became a workaholic, worked obsessively to avoid making mistakes because I did not believe in my own abilities, was afraid to make mistakes, and created a fast track to success because I believed that to be the only route to prosperity and success.

I also picked up many graduate degrees, including a doctorate, while I kept trying to prove to myself "that I was intelligent", despite actually believing the opposite as my high school teacher had declared when I was in his high school home room.

In this maze of conflicting thoughts and fear, I had lost myself. My wife took the route of parties and drugs as an escape mechanism while therapeutically working closely with Viet Nam veterans. I took the avenue of material and earth success.

It shouldn't have been a surprise when the divorce happened. Looking back, it is easy to see how my fears (a lack of belief in my own abilities/ a lack of self-esteem and self-confidence, the belief that I needed to work excessively to have money; and my belief in lack rather than abundance) all came into play in the failure of the marriage. While I was not the only one to contribute to the divorce, I certainly contributed mightily.

The divorce produced loneliness. I felt separated and questioned whether I would ever find someone to love who could also genuinely love me. I feared that perhaps I was destined to live my life alone and lonely. It took me a long time to discover and gain the strength of *solitude*, the peace that comes from within; where we can be happy and content with ourselves whether we are with someone else or not.

Due to the divorce, or perhaps because of it, I worked even more feverishly, was successful in my work career, and received numerous promotions. However, instead of reinforcing my intelligence and capabilities, each promotion caused me to further question my lack of abilities and belief in myself, because I now believed I had to be "somehow conning my superiors" and really didn't believe I deserved the promotions despite my wanting them.

Those fear-laden, erroneous thought patterns, further reinforced my childhood belief in fear of authority because I knew that since I was supposedly conning my superiors, it would only be a matter of time before they discovered my incompetence and would fire me. Accordingly, I had to work harder and harder and harder while doing what I considered to be absolutely perfect work, not daring to make a mistake, in order to keep this superflux going while receiving more and more responsibilities and raises.

Despite these fears, I accepted each new job because I wanted the fame and monies. I also worked hard to get additional graduate-level degrees because I had to *"prove to myself"* that I truly was intelligent - in order to overcome the fear, I had accepted from my high school teacher, that I was not smart enough to go to college. It resulted in me getting numerous master degrees, a degree in the ministry, a doctorate, and several other advanced certifications in such disciplines as organizational development, value engineering, change management, economics, marketing, and real estate over the years.

I find it absolutely fascinating how steadfast we defend, and then hold on to false, misperceived, fearful things as adults – *which we had accepted while we were young and immature* - despite being older and supposedly more mature.

That was certainly true for me as I responded to my high school teacher's assertion that I was "*not smart enough to go to college.*" Even though I have worked diligently to remove that fear over the years, it still periodically pops up at the very depth of the taproot level of that fear. When it does, it just simply means that I need to take the time to once again cleanse it from my consciousness. And, I do.

Instead of sweeping childhood fears/limitations out the door when we become an adult, our tendency, regardless of our age, is to grant them the ability to fester and grow into full-blown fear realities within the adult world we now inhabit. At least, that is what I had done, for more years than I like to admit.

Illustratively, my propensity for swearing and using foul language was based on a false, fearful belief that I was not as strong as others, and therefore had to be a "tough guy" if others were going to respect me as a leader. That false belief/machismo also led me to become addicted to coffee and cigarettes to force myself to stay aware for long hours so I could achieve any assignment I had been given, regardless of how unrealistic it may have been, in terms of time or scope. It also led me to nearly become a full-fledged alcoholic.

Using this example, the toxic, compounding ethos of fear is that regardless of how many promotions or raises you may receive, if your core belief/thought pattern is in a lack of self-confidence coupled with a belief in scarcity (the fear of "not having enough") then those are the thought patterns that *must manifest* in your world despite other successes!

Why? Because it is the Spiritual Law. And, the universe always operates according to spiritual laws.

For me, those destructive thought patterns became, "the more money I made, the more money I believed I had to make, just to survive". Those thoughts then compounded to create new fears such as believing my "luck" at continually being promoted would eventually run out, I would likely be fired for incompetence, and I would end up losing the money I had acquired.

Remember the Spiritual Law: Like Attracts Like

I was a classic example of how this spiritual law works: As long as I had this belief in scarcity or fear of abundance, I had to keep attracting things to me that would negatively impact the prosperity I was gaining. In other words, as always, the Law of the Universe would respond to *what I believed, not to what I hoped*.

In my situation, I lost money in the stock market, was conned out of money by those who made their living conning others, and was sued through a lawsuit that lacked justifiable merit.

Thank goodness, the Spiritual Law also works in such a manner that the moment you change your belief in scarcity, and come to BELIEVE you are deserving of the abundance and prosperity of the universe, then abundance will flow into your world – and *- it will stay in your world - as long as you believe it!*

This spiritual law informs us that unless we identify and clear our fears, those fearful thought patterns will continue to attract those things in the earth plane that will negatively impact us in our fear areas!

And, it will continue to do so - until we finally choose to use the strengths, we have at our disposal to clear those fears and remove them forever from our consciousness.

Fortunately, I was able to do so by developing *a new belief,* a new strength, that *God loves those who are prosperous*, and wants all of us to be abundant.

To verify that *God is abundance*, loves prosperity, and wants us all to have abundance; all we have to do is look at the unlimited number of leaves that God has placed on a tree, or the infinite blades of grass on a lawn, or the number of drops of water in the ocean, or the infinite grains of sand in a beach. These are testimonials to the reality of God's loving abundance.

EXERCISE 5

If You have a Challenge with Prosperity

I would like you to again pull out your spiritual journal if you have an issue with economic prosperity or even with abundance in general. Even if you don't, this is a fabulous exercise in learning more about your Creative Source. Regardless, this will be an excellent exercise for you to complete.

Sit down on a lawn at your home if you have one, or at a park that has trees in it. Reach your hand into the lawn and pick a handful of grass. Hold it in your hand and begin to count the number of individual blades of grass that are in your hand. When you finish, pick up another handful and do the same thing one more time. Once you have finished, keep this number in your mind and write it down in your spiritual journal.

Then look over the lawn or park where you are sitting. Begin to multiply how many individual hands- full of grass and individual blades of grass are in the park. It will be staggering. Candidly you won't be able to do it because the number will be so immense that your mind won't be able to comprehend it.

Then begin to do the same with the closest tree that is in bloom. Concentrate your vision on one branch, and begin to count the individual leaves on that branch. When you complete that task, then do the same with another branch, and then another. Once you realize the number of leaves is too large for you to continue to count, then stop, and realize how many leaves there still must be on this tree that you haven't yet counted.

Then, allow your mind to expand and consider how many leaves must be on all the trees in the park where you are sitting, in the city or farm where you live, in your state, your country, the world.

Let that number stagger you - because it will!

Then, realize that your Creative Source is even more bountiful than this.

When you finish this exercise, sit and contemplate how bountiful, abundant, the universe really is.

Since God is never wasteful, then how could God waste all of this unlimited beauty, if the Energy of God is not in total abundance? The simple answer is it could not!

This is a fabulous exercise to help you better understand the Creative Source that created you, along with the total unlimitedness, that God truly is. It will also dramatically expand your thinking as you realize this is the beauty and abundance of God Itself, the Divine Source that you think into.

△

God loves each of us as its own unique creation, and wants each of us to be abundant –not to be stuck "in a world where we only have lack and poverty", or "only have enough to get by with." God does not want us to have to live in a world of "almost enough", when we can have "more than enough". God's preference would be for each of us to live in a world where we have more than enough so we can have ample and can freely share it with others.

However, God has left that choice up to each of us with our own free will.

We may have, *not enough; barely enough; enough, more than enough; or abundance.* It is our choice. And, it will manifest as we believe it to be.

As far as God is concerned it is our birthright to be abundant and prosperous, and we do not have to work ridiculously long-hours, or hard labor to earn, or keep, the abundance that is that birthright.

While this discussion may appear to be exclusively focused on prosperity versus scarcity, it is a much larger discussion than that. Instead, it is valid in reference to all of our fears, regardless of what subject we may list them under.

Once we identify the fears, regardless of what they may be, and accept *that the only reason* those fears have manifested is so we can heal them and remove them from our world, we are well on our way home.

Then, the more we can come to accept the total unlimitedness of our Creative Source as also being our parent, from whom we can never be separate, we are more than halfway home. All we have to do is to put the belief into practice.

At that point, we can go about healing the identified fears by changing the thought pattern that caused them to manifest in the first place. As we do, *they will, and must, disappear into the nothingness from which they came!* This is another non-changing Spiritual Law.

As I looked back, it was not difficult to see how I had taken my childhood fears and *expanded them* into much larger fears in my adult life. Fortunately, along the way, I also began to manifest the true gifts and strengths that had resided within me from the time I was born, my divine spiritual self, as I loosened my fears so they could begin to be freed.

For example, following the divorce, I went to therapy and began to take a new inventory of who I was and what I had become. That process helped to start me on a new pathway, one with more positive thoughts and less fear.

Frequent discussions with my aunt and her metaphysical beliefs also became important developmental stones for me in my progress, along with my Rosicrucian studies. In addition, I began the process of beginning to understand how fear, itself, was holding me back from claiming the strengths which were already mine by right of my divine birth and conception.

Along the way, I came to understand, and more importantly, *accept*, that I was intelligent, I did have the ability to succeed without having to work myself to death.

I learned my intelligence was not in the form of earth defined IQ, but rather in being able to strategically envision things that needed to happen in the future to be successful, and then, possessing the ability to understand what actions needed to take place today, to help myself and others successfully manifest that future.

Over time, those strengths included helping prosperous businesses further improve themselves, as well as helping hurting businesses economically turn- themselves around.

And just like that, my career focus began to shift. I could rely upon and use my new skills, my new strengths, which I was in the process of allowing to emerge. I *no longer needed my old fears in my world: I could let them go.*

In other words, I was taking charge of *creating* my own NEW world! I was creating my own destiny.

During this process, I discovered that *the more fears I conquered - the more strengths I realized I had.*

It is a psychological reality that your blanket of fear *will cover up and keep your strengths* hidden under the quilt of heaviness from all those fears - until you can begin *to see and accept* that you already possess these strengths as part of your natural inner magnificent core. They are not something you have to make up or create since they have always been a natural part of who and what you are due to your divine conception. They have simply been hidden.

In other words, many of your strengths will remain hidden from your view, even though they are already there, until you allow them to more and more emerge as you heal your fears.

For me, my new strengths and abilities manifested into new belief patterns such as the new thought pattern that I could, and would be successful at whatever I did, regardless of whether I had to go around, under, or over the preverbal brick wall. No longer was a wall going to remain an impediment, or barrier, for me. With the new knowledge I was gaining, I now realized the wall was simply something to be overcome. It was but a temporary impediment that would allow my newly acquired skills and strengths to emerge.

This belief, grounded in spiritual truth, as well as in proven experiences, resulted in the brand-new enthusiasm and excitement for life which I acquired, and still hold, to this day.

You are surrounded and immersed in divine energy

This new awareness led me to the belief that *everything* is energy, regardless of whether it is a person, a business organization, a building, or a mountain. *Everything is alive and vibrates with the energy of our Creative Source.*

For example, a human body vibrates with strong positive energy when it is healthy. In contrast, it emits low or very limited energy when it is ill.

The same is true with a business organization and everything else. When a person is in fear, their energy vibration is very low. Therefore, according to the spiritual law of the universe, like a magnet, they must attract more fearful experiences to themselves. In contrast, when they elevate their energy vibration, they can reverse the cycle and when they do, they must attract the positive to themselves.

This is why the teachings in this book and in the fear-clearing trilogy are so powerful and important. When you are on your spiritual path and are growing spiritually, your energy vibration increases exponentially. It is not something you have to do to make it happen because it just happens naturally. In contrast, when you are walking the path of earth, the path of fear and limitation, your energy vibration is lower and it, therefore, must attract those things which are of a lesser energy frequency in vibration.

Again, it is not that one path is right and the other path wrong; because there is no right or wrong; since both are paths of learning. Rather, it is what you choose to have in your world. If you choose to have more fear, more debt, more injustice, more guilt, less loving relationships and increased ill health, then continue to walk the path of earth because that is what the earth path corresponds with.

In contrast, when you walk the spiritual path, you must attract goodness into your world as you clear your fears and walk free with high vibrational energy encircling your entire essence and being that occurs naturally as a result of your increased spiritual growth.

Again, the more fear you carry with you the more you become the magnet to attract more and more fear to yourself. The more fear you clear, the more you become the powerful magnet that will automatically draw more and more and more of your good to you. This is how natural the laws of the universe work.

A hurting business has low energy

The same is true with an economically hurting business organization. The more fear it has, the lower the energy level becomes, and the more the business results worsen. The worse the results become; the more fear is created and intensified.

Soon, the organization fills itself with nothing but fearful energy. The downward cycle is strongly perpetuated as innovation, creativity, and the former "can do" attitude the business used to possess, disappears. If the cycle is not changed, and the business redesigned, the organization will soon find itself in a death spiral.

The paradigm of employee power in business has completely reversed itself in recent years, especially since the economic downturn of 2008. Prior to that downturn, businesses-controlled employees and they could essentially be hired or fired at will. Since 2008, the paradigm has dramatically changed. Today, employees can change jobs on a whim and usually earn even more money when they do.

In today's work environment, employees start out looking for more *meaningful*, or *purposeful work*, when they begin a job search. They then end up accepting another job, usually with more money, in the hopeful anticipation that they are accepting a more meaningful job.

I suggest you also become aware that there is a larger element at play than simply being an employee resignation movement, or a job, or career shift, which is taking place here. The employee resignation trend is but another aspect of the *divine discontent* movement which is sweeping the planet as we clear more of our fears and increasingly move closer to the New Age of Compassion and Enlightenment.

Each of us will experience more and more *divine discontent* which is a feeling from within that keeps gnawing away, reminding us that we do have a *purpose*, an objective, a *meaningful goal* – and that is to learn about and express our spiritual unlimitedness. This is the only reason we are onearth at this time and space. To become increasingly aware of who and what we are spiritually, while learning to increasingly express it in thoughts and actions.

We can continue to attempt to ignore it if we choose because that is our right due to Free Will. However, *divine discontent* will continually return as it attempts to inspire us to move in this direction at this time when earth and we both so desperately need to learn to release and heal our fears, and in their place, rise to the spiritual height of our being while helping to heal all who are in our presence.

A priceless lesson

I also learned another priceless lesson during this process: All of the divine positive energy the Intelligence Source of the Universe has created, and has made available, is at my disposal.

It is Mine. I may choose to use it as I choose to use it – either in fear - or in creating the constructive things I want in my world regardless of whether it be health, abundance, loving relationships; or all three.

My new thought patterns, skills, and strengths included a be-lief that we can change anything we want to change, when, and as, we reduce and subsequently remove our fears.

These new thought patterns led to my successful transition into eight different careers- thus far. A friend once told me *"It takes a lot of courage to step into a new career and to do it success-fully".*

I had never thought of it in that way before. However, once I did, I realized that *courage* was also a new strength of mine, and I quickly added it to my inventory of strengths.

Another important thing for you to be aware of on your spir-itual journey to removing fear is that when you are spiritually receptive, God will send messengers to you with important learn-ings such as what happened with my new insight that courage is a strength of mine which I had not previously been aware of.

In other words, the more we learn to be receptive and listen, the higher the increase in our spiritual energy, the stronger our spiritual messages and guidance will become along with their frequency.

The fact is that all good learnings or teachings come from God. If those teachings or those words are meant for you, the Creative Source will figure out how to get those messages to you for your learning and personal growth.

Sometimes they will come through unlikely sources such as what happened with the gentleman that told me how much cour-age it takes to successfully create a new career, while other times they will come from different sources. However, regardless of when or how they come, rest assured if the message is right for you, it will somehow be delivered to you.

Your spiritual messages, or answers to the questions or prayers you are requesting will come from other people. The reason is that God uses this avenue as a reinforcement that all people are inherently good and all are a part of the energy and substance that is the Divine Source of all existence.

As I grew and removed more and more fear, my new strengths continued to manifest. For example, they expanded to include a new belief in writing skills which I didn't believe I previously possessed but which I am now using to write this book; a new self-confidence and belief in myself and my abilities that regardless of whatever I approached it would be successful; a belief that collaboration and teamwork in management were far superior to any autocratic style; my new belief in abundance; and an understanding that no fears are stronger than the God I believe in.

This is not to suggest that everything went swimmingly well without challenges.

Since we choose to create challenges to help us grow spiritually, I certainly chose to create many, many of those kinds of challenges, or opportunities for growth, along my path. Illustratively, I have been laid off; threatened to be fired; promoted; sued; criticized as being ignorant and stupid; praised as being brilliant; judged and accused of being an arrogant, manipulative, egotistical leader; and praised as a team-oriented, sensitive, manager of people.

In retrospect, each of those experiences, not all of which have been what I would describe as fun, have led to incredible growth on my part in finding and expressing the gifts of who and what I truly am.

Those experiences have allowed me to successfully transform and reinvent myself in eight different careers, and to be successful, in each. I have gained self-confidence and truly believe in my own capabilities and decision-making without arrogance, and hopefully, am still sufficiently humble to be able to continue to learn from others.

I have removed my fear of God and have in its place discovered and believe in my God of intelligence, abundance, healing, love, and total unlimitedness. I have also gained *financial freedom* which is the true definition of prosperity.

In turn, I bless each and every one of these experiences because without them I never would have been able to discover the beauty of who I truly am, and I would not have had the opportunity to express that beauty in this lifetime. This is why I thank God each day and stand in gratitude when I awaken each morning that I have the opportunity this day to discover and express even more of the inner magnificence in which my God has created me.

Was I scared during the time I was laid off, or sued, or criticized, or judged? Absolutely!

As a matter of fact, being wrongfully sued and publicly accused of wrong-doing was absolutely terrifying to me.

It meant that what I had spent years accumulating could potentially be taken away from me. It was not until I realized that no one can take anything away from me – *except me* – that I was able to change my fear vibration from one of negativity into positive outcomes.

Sometimes I was so scared, that I had trouble even getting out of bed. It felt as if I was being strangled by my own fears. But there are also so many previously unknown strengths and abilities that each of us possesses.

To be obsessed by, and controlled or dominated by fear, or even by a particular fear – and then to be able to take control of that fear and change it into the positive – not only for ourselves but for our world - is an incredibly positive and uplifting experience. *It is also the definition of Courage* – which I learned I possessed!

I want to quickly add that there is a likelihood that some, or at least part of all of the negative things that have been said about me in judgment, may have been true about me at one point in my life. However, what I also know is that I am always in the process of change.

Who I was yesterday, does not define me, or mean, that is who I am, or will be, tomorrow!

I also know, today, that I no longer have to accept another person's judgment of me or that of earth's judgment, as being the truth. In contrast, it is what *I believe myself to be* - that is true – *for me*.

It is only *what I believe about myself* that I will express in my world.

EXERCISE 6

Fears and Limitations You have Kept and Added to as an Adult

As previously indicated, most of us keep the fears and beliefs in limitations into our adulthood that we accepted as a youngster. It is also likely that you added even more fears as you have lived additional years on earth and have had earth and its institutions teach you even more limitations that you supposedly had to accept.

Accordingly, I would now like you to identify what you believe those fears and limitations to be and write them down in your spiritual journal.

As before, do not judge yourself. Do not be critical of yourself. Your only responsibility in writing these things down in your spiritual journal is to be as honest with yourself as you can possibly be. That is their value.

As you do this, you will discover more and more about yourself and the fears you have expanded and added to as you have walked earth through the first twenty-some years of your life. Again, it is highly unlikely that you have ever previously examined your fears and limitations under the microscope; as you are currently doing so you can clear them from your consciousness.

EXERCISE 7

Strengths You have kept, Expanded, and Added as an Adult

Our next exercise is essentially the same process, except that in this exercise, you are being asked to identify and describe in detail, all of the strengths you have developed and/or expanded since your childhood. Write these down in your spiritual journal and keep adding to it over time as you learn more and more about yourself and all of the strengths you have brought with you this lifetime.

List all of the new strengths that come to your attention. Do not be modest. Become expansive as you honestly take an inventory of all the abilities and strengths you possess. Remember, you always have more strengths than you need to overcome and conquer your fears and limiting thoughts. Describe as many of these as you can think of.

If you are having difficulty with this exercise, remember that God, an unlimited God, an all-loving God, has created YOU. Who and what do you believe this Divine Source has created? One or two strengths, or many, many strengths and assets?

Again, write every one of these in your spiritual journal.

When you completed the exercises from the previous chapter, you developed an understanding of the fears and the strengths you brought into your youth from prior lives as a baby - so you could heal them this lifetime.

The exercises from this chapter are designed to give you the opportunity to update your self-diagnosis, as the adult you are today, so you can more accurately assess who and what you are in terms of your existing fears and strengths.

This self-diagnosis process, and the examples I have candidly shared with you using the fears and strengths I identified when I was using this process, have been designed to help you sincerely look at yourself, so you can determine if you are comfortable with who and what you are - *today* – or whether you want to change what you have become through your thought patterns.

If you are completely and undeniably comfortable with who you are today, then there is no longer a need for you to continue with this book.

However, if you desire to make some necessary changes, as I did, then I suggest you continue reading and doing.

Remember – *You* have the power to *change* the world you have created, and live in today, as well as to transform yourself as you desire.

In the next chapter, we will examine change and what is associated with creating change within yourself as well as in your individualized world.

TRANSFORM YOURSELF

"If you know the enemy and know yourself you need not fear the results of a hundred battles".

—Sun Tzu

As indicated in the last chapter, I had allowed myself to be riddled with fear and limited thought patterns for many years of my youth, which continued into adulthood. Despite the fact that others may have looked at me and the world I had created – and defined it successful – I knew different.

It was not until I had reached a point in my life where I was able to become aware of how completely I had allowed myself to be blanketed by fear that I was able to initiate change and begin to limit the rippling and insidious grip of those fears. As I did, I discovered I was able to start the process to reverse the negative fear vibrations I had tightly wrapped around myself. It was at that time that I could also begin to release the inner power of who and what I AM.

But to accomplish this required that I momentarily step back from my earth fears and begin to glimpse my true self. My true self is the I AM of my existence (the spiritual being of who and what each of us is inside which is the constant linkage with our Creative Source). The I AM is that all-powerful mantra from our Creative Source that instructs us to speak the words I AM for whatever it is that we desire. When we speak the I AM, we are speaking from our Divine Self. The I AM is also the secret name for God.

We then determine the words that follow the I AM, as we set about creating, or changing our world. For example, I AM abundance, I AM health, I AM loved. As we use these words they must manifest as long as we believe the words we speak after the I AM. The time frame for manifestation is predicated upon how many layers of fear need to be cleared for the substance we have requested to manifest in material form.

The same is true if we use negative words with our I AM. Illustratively, when we speak the words to the universe that I AM poor, I AM broke, I am miserable, I AM unhappy, I AM sick, I AM lonely, those are the words that the universe must respond to. You can have health, or you can have illness. You can be abundant, or you can be in poverty. But you can't have both.

In other words, you cannot have happiness in your world when you are claiming unhappiness. You have the power to choose and to make whatever changes you wish whenever you want to do so.

Look at the words you are using today. Are you using the I AM for positive change in your world or are you continuing to reinforce the negative limiting aspects and thoughts in your world?

Your words are incredibly powerful and they create what you request and believe, because you are in control of your individualized world.

Be careful that you are not claiming one thing with your I AM, and then voiding it with other words you are using. For example, when you speak your claim to the universe that *I AM Abundance*, be careful that you don't later start talking with an acquaintance and tell them, *"How broke"* you are.

The two are in conflict. Your conflicting words place the universe in the position of not knowing whether to respond to your request to stay in poverty or to manifest abundance. Therefore, it will keep in place your existing condition, which is your predominant thought pattern of poverty, despite your speaking words of abundance in your affirmation.

In contrast, rather than telling your acquaintance how broke you are, and thereby affirming that condition of poverty to the universe, I suggest you use words to describe your existing condition such as, "temporarily, I am finding myself with a lack of money, but I know that that condition is in the process of changing". That type of wordage removes the conflict and frees the universe to manifest what you are requesting which is economic prosperity.

The self-diagnosis or inventory process illustrated in the previous exercises helped me hold a mirror in front of my face so I could see how frightened I had become through a lack of self-confidence in my own abilities, fear of criticism, belief in lack, and fear of authority figures. That mirror, together with a beginning belief that I did not need to continue to be dominated by fear, gave me the ability to begin to step out of my fears and

and make the necessary changes I needed to make so I could begin to clear them.

Like a magnet, once you begin the process of clearing your fears, more fears will be attracted to you so you can also clear them. Soon, you will discover that the beginning process of clearing your fears will become natural. It will then become a permanent part of your living. And, I assure you, the more fears you cleanse yourself from, the more your life will change for the better.

This is the reason I chose to share the process with you and was willing to use myself as an example despite knowing that some people who have known me would have difficulty envisioning me with the words that I used. That is how good I think I used to be at camouflaging my fears and anxieties so I could hide them from others.

It has been my experience that camouflaging or hiding oneself from the world is not that unusual. Instead, I have found that the vast majority of people have become adept at camouflaging themselves from the outer world while attempting to hide their fears and insecurities. It just seems to be the way of the earth to operate in that manner.

The taking inventory and assessment process, along with the divorce, provided me the opportunity to seriously consider making personal changes. Fortunately, I chose to do it despite it being scary.

The interesting thing about change is that generally, we don't just change on a whim. Instead, we usually need a dramatic event to seriously consider making major changes. It may be a nasty break-up, a divorce, the death of a loved one, an economic disaster such as losing our job, being evicted, or becoming seriously ill – to create a major inner desire – *that we must change.*

I call this *Dissatisfaction with how things are.* In my case, it was my divorce that served as the catalyst to begin this re-examination process. The self-diagnosis tools helped me further the desire, while holding up a mirror of self-assessment to let me clearly see how insecure I had become as the result of being driven by fear.

The desire to change can also be as simple as picking up this book and becoming aware that you don't have to continue to live your life the way in which you have. Or, it could be as simple as realizing that while God loves the janitor who cleans floors and the maid who changes beds and cleans toilets, God also loves those who are abundant and prosperous; so why not choose to be abundant?

God loves those who are healthy and those who are ill; those who are lonely, and those who are loved. So why not choose to be abundant, healthy, and loved?

God constantly and continually loves you and stands with you regardless of what you believe, or what you have created in your world.

God is happy as long as you are happy.

God always sees you as your Divine, unlimited Self, and stands ready to put the power of the universe behind you whenever you desire to change and express more of the unlimited being that you already are.

It all depends on what you want to create in the world in which you live. It is up to you and me since each of us is the Creative Source for our individual worlds.

Change can begin to occur at the point in time when we tell ourselves that we cannot continue to function in the way we are currently living.

It can be a time when we say to ourselves that we are at our wit's end. We have tried everything and nothing seems to be working right, so we had better consider doing something different – and do it quickly – or we are going to lose who we are, along with everything we have become!

I firmly believe these are the times when we have the opportunity to make *serious changes*.

This reflection point is what I refer to as SPIRITUAL TIME!

It is an opportunity for each of us to reawaken our spiritual selves while we are on earth – that part of us we naturally express between lives while we are living *beyond earth* – before we return to the earth plane of existence. This is the part of our God's Essence that is without fear and does not believe in limitations.

It is also the time when we can take our beliefs and our thought patterns, and actually *apply* them. When we do, we will see their *"real power"* in action. That is the time when your beliefs transition from being what you "think" they may be conceptually, or theoretically, and they will become *real to you*!

It is only when you begin to use the power that is *the real you* – that *you* will discover *the true power that you already are*!

Once you begin to discover this power that is at your disposal, no one, can ever again, take it away from you!

However, it requires that no matter how anxious or frightened you may be, you are the only one who can, and who has to take the first step *in faith, in courage,* to begin the journey to your spiritual freedom.

People tend to put their faith in other people. Unfortunately, when they do, they can frequently be disappointed.

In contrast, when you place your faith in God – you cannot, and will not, fail!

Illustratively, we may say to ourselves that "*nothing is more powerful than God*", and theoretically, we may think we mean it. However, it does not become more than an academic concept until we actually *use that belief,* and see it manifest in our world, that it will actually *become real to you.* At that point, and only at that point, does it become "owned" by you, and no longer conceptual.

Make your own demonstration of faith

When you experience a personal demonstration from using your own God Power, you will have your own personal testimonial of how real God's power, *you,* actually are.

From that point forward, forever, your belief that *no fears are more powerful than God* will become, perpetually, a part of you, fully integrated into your essence and being. This new belief will become a major component of who and what you are emerging and transforming yourself into being.

Never again will you *hope* this belief is *real* – because you will *personally know* it is real!

It was not until I examined my old spiritual beliefs, made changes, and began to get rid of my old limiting thought patterns – that I was able to replace them with new, powerful, unlimited beliefs. Two of these were critically important to me. I used them consistently during this process and still do today in one form or another.

I share them with you:

1. My God is more powerful than anything I feared, and

2. My *God wants me to be intelligent, inspired, abundant, happy, and healthy!"*

As I began to apply these two new beliefs to my old fears, I discovered that My God truly *was more powerful than the fears I had held* for so long, and that My God truly did desire for me to release and use my intelligence and my divine inspiration, to become abundant, happy and healthy.

As a result, my new strengths began to emerge as my old fears began to dissipate.

As I continued to apply these new beliefs, I cleared more and more of my old fears. They did not all magically disappear overnight. However, I could quickly see progress and had demonstrable proof for myself that God works miracles.

I also learned that I was continually developing a deeper appreciation, respect, and love for who and what my God became to me in contrast to the old fear-laden beliefs I had developed and carried about God from my days of formalized religion.

I also discovered that the more fears I cleared, the more of my new strengths emerged. Like magic. The more fear I cleared, the more strengths I discovered I had and could exhibit in my world; and the more abundance, happiness and health I exhibited.

I still use this process today to continue to clear out the tap-root of fears I undoubtedly still carry with me, or as new and different fears try to jump into my world.

It is fun and exciting. It makes life interesting and refreshing. I discovered that the more enthusiasm I exhibited for the life I was living, the more excited I became to see what new strengths I had, and could use each and every day.

For example, today, I love writing and seeing my talent in using words. This is a skill set I never thought I had. I love it. It excites me. It thrills me.

I find I also still have a passion for building beautiful new environmentally-friendly residential homes. I love it and it still excites me. I will continue doing so until it no longer thrills me. Then, I will have the opportunity to do something else that is new if I choose to do so.

This is the beauty of what my God is presenting me – an open smorgasbord of unlimited goodies – from which I may choose!

I look forward to waking up every day to the new world that greets me. This is the personal learning and enthusiasm I awaken to every single day.

It was never this way for me when I was driven by fear and woke up every morning to fearful negative thoughts. Today I am excited to wake up. Previously, I woke up to my same old world where I drearily had to continually combat my demons.

Perhaps this is why I have successfully transformed and re-created myself in eight different careers – so far.

I have found that life can be incredibly exciting as long as I allow it to be. I love waking up each day and discovering how life is ready to greet me. The first thing I do, every morning upon waking, is to thank my God for being alive so I have this new day of excitement to experience the earth and to discover more about who I AM.

I also affirm that God is the only thing that exists in my world and that God is my Creative Source. Therefore, I am the health, the love, the abundance, the inspiration, the guidance, the enthusiasm for life that my God is. At that point, I am ready to optimistically begin my day.

I also came to the awareness that God has created me to be a miniature Creative Source of Power in my own personal world. As God thought and created the earth and all of the galaxies we live in, this same Creative Source created me with all of Its own attributes of love and goodness.

In other words, I have all of the same attributes as my Creative Source, except I only have them in miniature form. I was not the vast ocean that God is. However, I am a drop of water within that ocean. Therefore, I contain all the attributes, the same DNA that God possesses. The only distinction is that mine are in miniature form.

In other words, it is up to me to determine what I want to have manifest in the individual world that I am responsible for creating – my fears – or my belief in unlimited goodness from my Creative Source.

It is always my choice! This is the power of free will or free agency that God has given each of us.

I also want to share with you that all of my fears did not instantly disappear once I embarked upon this process. Nor are they supposed to. *It is a life-long learning process.* That is the reason we are living this earth life. We did not create all our fears in one day, and they will not all magically go away in one day.

However, once we begin the process of clearing our fears, *our life will change for the better.* There is absolutely no question about that.

The reason is that you will see and personally exhibit God in action.

If you are financially hurting, as you work to clear your fear about prosperity and claim your abundance as a child of an abundant God, you will begin to experience new opportunities for abundance manifesting.

It may be that you will find a five-dollar bill on the sidewalk to tell you that you are on the right path. It may be that you receive a refund in the mail. It may be that your budget stretches a little further this month than it did last month. It may be that you receive a promotion.

It doesn't matter how large or small these testimonials may be. They are God's way of reminding you to Remember that God is in charge of the universe, everything is in God's realm, and *it will be done unto you as you believe.* The more capacity you develop in a belief in abundance the more abundance you will attract!

Address the fear, change your beliefs, and allow God to show you the new direction. Your new direction will manifest as per your words and your belief.

As indicated, all the fears I had created did not magically disappear the day I started this journey. It was not until I began to work to clear specific fears, I knew I held; and saw the power in my new beliefs that God was more powerful than any fears I had;

and that God truly wanted me to be healthy, abundant, intelligent, and loved; that I saw those fears begin to shrink while my new strengths and skills emerged.

That was, and still is, the fun associated with this life-long journey of learning and experiencing.

The reason why we experience problems or challenges

Another thing I found on this journey is that we as human beings have a tendency to stay static, and not grow, as long we don't have challenges we need to respond to. *In other words, it is easier to not make change than it is to make change.*

This is the reason that the universe brings us growth opportunities along the way so we can allow our new skills and strengths to emerge. It happens like magic. I also choose to name these new episodes *Challenges* rather than *problems.*

Again, the power of the words we use is important. When the universe brings me something I need to deal with, I name it a Challenge and also immediately name it *good. That way, it must manifest as both.*

Accordingly, it will quickly allow me to use my strength to overcome the new challenge since the challenge is not nearly as large as it would be if I had named it a problem and bad, and given it all of that energy and power. I also know it is good because I had been presented with the opportunity to use my new strength to vanquish it.

I have also discovered that sometimes we can begin to clear a fear we have carried for a long time, and may even feel we have cleared it. Then, later that fear may pop up again in order for us to have the opportunity to ensure we clear it *at the taproot level*, forever, from our consciousness, instead of at the stem or blossom level.

Or, it may pop up in a different form simply so we can say to ourselves, "*Now this feels good. I no longer hold this fear* even though it has now appeared in this new form and format. Thank you, Father, that this is so."

New fears will naturally flow into your world as you clear them

That is what happened to me. The more fears I worked to clear, the more fears that over time seemed to naturally flow into my world to be cleared with the new strengths I acquired. Some of those experiences included being criticized, judged, terminated, fired and sued; but none of them meant that I was powerless.

Instead, as long as I believed that my God was more powerful than any of those fear incidents – and as long as I had the courage to continue to believe and apply the Spiritual Beliefs and Laws – I was, and would always – be fine.

As a matter of fact, I always turned out far, far better than I had been prior to the manifestation of those new fears. Illustratively, I found myself moved into new careers, new abundance, new health, and new relationships.

As long as we allow our Creative Source to be in charge, we will always prevail, and come out on top of all of our fears.

The reason is that we allow our magnificent inner self to emerge is because we are the offspring, the children of an all-powerful loving God; and our God will never take us halfway.

TWO DIVERGENT ROADS

"Do the thing you fear to do and keep on doing it... that is the quickest and surest way ever yet discovered to conquer fear".

—Dale Carnegie

Once you gain this new knowledge regarding the power of your inner being, you have one of two choices:

1. You can put your new knowledge into action, and prove, that it can be used to transform your life.

2. Or, second, you can attempt to forget what you have learned and try to revert to your old patterns and way of living.

The choice is yours and yours alone. If you choose to try to forget and return to your old behavior patterns you will discover that a *divine discontent* will begin to seep into your consciousness. This will occur when your divine inner being, coupled with your new spiritual knowledge, attempts to inspire you to choose the right path to walk.

Since God has given you free will, or the will to choose what it is that you want in your world, you don't necessarily need to listen to this inner divine voice.

However, if you choose to walk down that alternate pathway, I warn you that your divine disconnect will continue to gnaw at you now that you know the spiritual truth about who and what you are – and the magnificence that you are able to become and express; until you again begin to consider experiencing the spiritual truth you have learned about who and what you are.

This inner urging will become even stronger when you find yourself standing at a *fork in the road* and you discover yourself *vacillating* regarding which road to take.

My suggestion is to listen to your inner voice during this period of indecisiveness as it will always attempt to guide you in the right direction.

The American poet, Robert Frost, wrote his famous poem "The Road Not Taken" in regard to this type of indecisiveness. He beautifully narrated the situation we face when we stand at the fork in the road and debate which road to take as he expressed in poetic words *"Two roads diverged in a yellow wood, and sorry I could not travel both, and be one traveler, long I stood and looked down one as far as I could to where it bent in the undergrowth..."*

Frost believed that making a single decision and choosing the correct road versus the opposite one can dramatically transform your life.

I wholeheartedly agree with him.

Based on personal experience, I found that when I chose to take the path of clearing my fears, I made a decision that allowed me to recreate my life and become who and what I am today.

In contrast, if I would have chosen to take the divergent road, I would have continued to be who and what I had been to that point in my life. That person and the behavior they expressed was not one I cherished, or felt best represented, who I had the potential to become.

Frost continued his poem and added, "*Two roads diverged in a wood, and I, I took the one less traveled by, and that has made all the difference*".

The theme of Frost's poem is that human beings are defined by the options they face, and the choices they make. Frost was spot on.

Illustratively, you are defined by the choices you make *now* that you have come to the point in your life *where you have earned the right* to learn the truth about who and what you are spiritually and the power you have at your disposal, regardless of what you may choose to do with it.

You can walk a path of unbridled enthusiasm and excitement if you choose to clear your fears and allow your divine inner abilities to spread their wings and like the most powerful magnet attract beauty, goodness, and unlimitedness into your life.

Or, you can define yourself by choosing to return to your old patterns, and travel the road where the majority of mankind have walked for centuries, because it closely resembles the ways of earth, and appears to be easier and less troublesome.

The road of earth is *the road of obedience* while *the spiritual road is paved with self-discipline*.

When you choose to walk the path that clears your fears and allows your inner magnificence to be expressed you will be choosing a spiritual road that is *far less traveled by your fellow man*.

However, it is also the one where you can be freed from mental and emotional bondage, and where you will find yourself with self-confidence and self-esteem, excitedly, living your life in absolute freedom.

Each one of us is currently going through a period of great change, no matter who we are, where we live, or where we work. It is as if everything which had previously been stable in our world has been thrown into a great blender so it can be stirred up. Regardless of what you pull out of the blender, whether it is a job or a fear of losing your job; health or the fear of catching Covid-19 or a variant; a loving relationship or being isolated; continued focus on the material or on spiritual substance; it is currently in a state of flux.

This is a good thing because the blender has been designed to help you choose between the divergent paths you may walk. Due to the many changes taking place, you clearly have numerous divergent paths and opportunities to choose from in numerous areas of your life, far more so than the vast majority of people who have ever lived on earth have previously faced.

Each choice, in one form or other, will force you to choose how you will deal with the God that you are now aware is within you, in your divine essence, waiting to be freed as you clear more and more of the fears which have enslaved you.

For example, the fork in the road depicts that one road you may take is the awareness of the *life* that you are, the unique and individual livingness that you possess which has been birthed by your Creative Source. That spiritual road will lead you to the awareness that God is a constant companion within you. Without God, you would fail to exist. Because the Creative Source is Life Itself, it can never fail to exist. Therefore, you will never fail to exist either.

Or, you could take the road of earth which would attempt to convince you that you have been created by a random error, caused somehow by some freak accident, which has taken place somewhere, in the universe.

When you begin to walk the spiritual road, you will come to the recognition that God is not only aware of you, but that you and God are One.

The road of earth is where God does not exist, God is not aware of you, you and God are separate, and you have come into being by a random accident.

Because of free will, it is your choice to choose which of the two roads you want to travel. There is no right or wrong. It is only what is right for you. If you choose the earth path to walk at this time, it will only mean that you will delay your spiritual path until later this life, or until a future life. Eventually, you, like all of us, will end up walking the spiritual path, but only you have the free will to decide when you decide to make that decision.

The spiritual road is where you recognize that the God within you has great knowledge of who *you* are. It is a personal and individualized connection that goes back to the very beginning when God thought into Itself, into a Love Thought, and you, together with all mankind and all life, were conceived within the context of this vibrational love energy.

You are constantly in God's awareness no matter what you do or say. If this were not so, you would not have *life*. If you choose to walk the spiritual road it will bring you to your knowledge of

RICHARD A. FELLER

the God within by recognizing the fact that you *live,* and that you have your uniqueness as an individual creation of your perfect Creative Source.

The next step on your spiritual road is to recognize that you have intelligence and that you are *intelligent.* Many of us fail to take the time to recognize the intelligence that we are as we either take it for granted or simply operate on the premise that others are more intelligent than we are. While everyone has intelligence, greater or lesser, everyone has intelligence because the God that is within everyone is *All Intelligence.*

God is Mind Itself. Remember, you always possess all the intelligence you ever need to achieve what you have come to accomplish. Never doubt that, because it is true.

As you think into the Mind of God you think into that part of Mind that corresponds to *your* interest and *your* mental focus. Think about that for a moment.

Everyone has different interests and focal points of emphasis. Accordingly, they think into the part of the Mind of God that most draws their interest, and in turn, they receive from the part of the Mind of God that most corresponds to them based upon that interest.

This is another example of *the spiritual law, Like Attracts Like,* in action.

You will find that as you walk this road there will be many common areas where you will seek God. Remember also that God is different for each person because every single individual is different unto themselves. That is the reason why no human being, not a single one of the 8.6 billion individuals living on our planet today, has the same DNA, or the same fingerprints. While that may sound preposterous, it is nevertheless true!

This is how unique God has made you, different from every other human being, regardless of whether they are living on earth at this time or are in another energy form elsewhere in existence.

On this particular road, you cannot borrow another God since your God looks and acts differently from the Gods of any other person in existence.

In other words, you reflect within yourself, what you believe your God to be, according to your beliefs.

Illustratively, if you believe your God is one that punishes, or one that seeks revenge, or one that is warlike; then this is the God who lives within you and it will be the God you express in your actions and behavior when you come into contact with others.

If you believe in a God of good, you will act out your God of good.

If you believe in a God of love, you will act out your God of love.

If you believe that your God is angry, then you will manifest this God in your anger.

If you believe God is unjust, then you will be unjust in your actions.

It is as simple, or as complex as that.

In other words, again, you will always be *what you believe you are* – not what *you really are* – but who and what you believe you are.

EXERCISE 8

Who and What is God to You Today?

I would again like to ask you to pull out your spiritual journal and prepare to write in it.

In order to help you to discover your God of Love on this spiritual pathway means that you must first recognize who and what your God is to you, today.

Accordingly, I ask that you write in your spiritual journal who and what you believe your God is to you today:

1.   Is it a God of anger?

2.   Is it a God of unjust?

3.   Is it a God of punishment?

4.   Is it a God of revenge?

5.   Is it a God of indifference?

6.   Is it a God of justice?

7.   Is it a God of Love?

8.   Is it a God of peace?

9.   Is it a God of intelligence?

10. Is it a God of gentleness?

Please add other answers as you identify what your God is to you. Also, remember to be honest with yourself and write down your answers to these questions regardless of how they may or may not sound. Remember, your spiritual journal is confidential and you can only grow spiritually by being honest with yourself.

This exercise is very important because who you believe your God to be is the God you express to others. Change what you believe God to be to you, and you will change what you believe yourself to be, and how you choose to express yourself to others.

EXERCISE 9

Who is the God to those People who Surround You?

The next step is to recognize who and what God is to those who surround you.

Draw a line down the middle of the page in your spiritual journal. On the left side write the name of the person you have identified, i.e., a parent. Then, on the right side of the page, write your description of who and what you believe their God is to them.

Continue to do this for the instrumental people in your world such as your spouse, relatives, teachers, or your boss.

Please be aware that by recognizing another's God, you are showing honor and respect for that individual, even though you are doing this confidentially in your private journal.

If their God is angry, allow them the right to be angry. If their God is unjust, allow them the right to be unjust. If their God is revenge, allow them the right to be vengeful.

In other words, don't expect them to be where you are in your spiritual growth journey. Instead, your goal is to try to be such a strong example of happiness, love, goodness, and gentleness; that observing you and how you interact and express yourself others, they will also desire to become more like the actions that you are expressing.

How they view their God will change. As it does, how they express their personal belief in their God with others, will also change.

You can only teach by example. You cannot teach by persuasion or argument. You do not have the ability to change anyone since they are the only ones who can choose to change themselves. Your only role is to honor them by knowing the truth for them, where they are today, while showing them a divergent path that they could choose to walk any time they desired to do so.

△

All of us know people who are very difficult to love or to even accept in our world. They are individuals who are admittedly very challenging to be around. If they are in your world, rest assured they are there for a specific reason. They are not there by accident, or by randomness.

For example, they may be in your world to teach you a spiritual lesson you need to learn even though it may be distasteful for you to learn it from them.

Or, it may be that they knew while *beyond earth, outside of the veil of earth,* that you would be in their life this time, and that you would be willing to teach them about a different road they could take, one that earth beings do not normally take; and that you would love them enough to provide them this knowledge through your own actions and your new behaviors.

Your role, on this *less traveled road* you are choosing to walk, is to become knowledgeable of the fact that those who are difficult to love are not deliberately attempting to be difficult or unlovable. Instead, they are attempting to live to the extent that they are capable of living with the knowledge, the fears, and the emotional pain they currently possess.

Your role is to say to yourself, privately and confidentially, "they are children who are simply acting out what they believe their God to be".

You don't ask a child to build a professionally designed skyscraper, to paint like Monet, or to perform musically like Mozart. Instead, you ask the child to use blocks to build a miniature building. If they don't do it correctly, you don't criticize them for not doing it perfectly. Instead, you applaud them for their attempt and teach them how to do it better the next time. Using this spiritually motivational technique, they will become responsive and eager to do it better the next time when they have the opportunity to do so.

It is the same when you find someone on the road you are now walking who is difficult. Genuinely praise them for what they are capable of being. By doing that you will inspire them to go higher.

Walking this path, you will come to the awareness that you will never want to expect or ask someone who is spiritually a child to instantly become a spiritual adult. That would be cruel and unfair.

Rather, you will learn to take them where they are and encourage them with your words and actions to grow spiritually, step-by-step, until they can become the spiritual adult, they are capable of becoming, based on the magnificence within themselves.

When you become aware of the God within someone who is a spiritual infant, you speak to them in a gentle way. You use honey with your words, and not vinegar. You still express what you feel the need to speak, but now you do it gently, instead of harshly as you would have done in the past.

This is the path you decided to take when you came to the fork in the road.

Even though it is less traveled on earth, this road will lead you to new found freedom, self-confidence, and enjoyment in everything that happens in your world, because you now know you are the only one who has created it, and if you desire, you are the only one with the power to change it.

All is waiting for you to decide what you truly want in your world – which path do you choose to walk for the rest of the time you have allocated to yourself to live here on earth?

WE ARE FORTUNATE TO BE LIVING ON EARTH NOW

"Don't be afraid to see what you see". —Ronald Reagan

Spiritually, we are fortunate to be living in this special time. The Age of Fear and Shaking, which has lasted for more than 5,000 years, is beginning to come to an end.

That is the reason fear is becoming so rampant today. When an age is coming to an end, the end of the purpose of that age, becomes so pronounced that we cannot hide from it any longer. In other words, it becomes so visible and in front of our faces that we realize we have no choice but to heal it.

That is what is happening now as the Age of Fear which has lasted on earth for so long is increasingly drawing to a close.

We are spending our lives on the cusp of entering a New Age, which is a rare occurrence. We are in the process of coming to an age where mankind will be living in compassion with one another, in peace and harmony, in enlightenment, and will be putting into practice the spiritual perfection in which we were created. The New Age we are referring to has been named the Age of Compassion, or the Age of Compassion and Enlightenment, by the spiritual masters.

However, to transition from the prior age into the new age, it will be necessary for mankind, as well as the earth, to make dramatic changes because without a spiritual or "chemicalization" process the New Age will not be able to manifest. It will require cleansing limitation thinking and the thick layers of fear mankind has created which have surrounded our planet over the many years in which man has walked on earth; and which have become increasingly thickened in the past 5,000 years.

The fact that we have chosen to live this particular lifetime on earth, at this specific moment, has not happened by accident or randomness.

Rather, we have chosen to come to earth and live our life during this unique time for two reasons:

1. To clear our own fears, and

2. As we do, to help earth heal itself by sharing the positive energy we send forth as our inner spiritual being emerges through our fear clearing process.

The positive vibrational energy released by our individual transformation process will have an incredible *accumulative effect* as it combines with the vibrations from others who are also concurrently cleansing themselves of fear. This newly-released positive energy *will mingle and integrate itself* within the spiritual energy currently being sent to earth to enable the New Age to more readily prepare to emerge.

When we were living *beyond earth,* while we were making our decisions concerning this lifetime, we asked to sign up for this task. Otherwise, we would not be living our lives in this particular time frame.

If I were to use an analogy, it would be to compare the earth to a bucket filled with clean water that has a thick layer of mud at the bottom. The mud is equivalent to all of the fears that have been created over the years since man first walked on this planet. The mud has become a thick layer of sludge and slime, the cumulative vibration of negativity that surrounds our planet, and which in turn, causes anxiety and limiting thoughts to be prevalent within our thinking patterns.

This accumulation of fear has crystalized into a thick layer of debris that clings to the bottom of the bucket because it is of such a heavy density. In order for the earth, and for each of us to start fresh, we need to allow our magnificent inner selves to emerge. As a result, it is necessary that the mud be cleared out of the bottom of the bucket.

Unfortunately, we aren't able to simply tip the bucket upside down and have it cleaned since the accumulated slush-pile of fear tenaciously clings to the bottom of the bucket, and it doesn't want to be disturbed, or even loosened, if it can possibly avoid it.

Accordingly, in order to clear the mud, it is necessary to fill the bucket with the mud with clean water, and then dump the bucket with the mud in it; over and over again; until the mud at the bottom of the bucket is finally released— and nothing is left - other than the resultant crystal clean water in the bucket.

This is called Spiritual *Chemicalization,* the *purging process,* analogous to the changes referred to by *ancient alchemists. This "chemicalization process"* is required to assist the earth clear out the mud, until the crystal clean water emerges throughout the entire bucket without any trace of the muddy debris.

In this manner, each of us will be contributing to the emergence of the manifestation of the Age of Compassion as we go through our own spiritual "chemicalization" process.

All of the things I am describing are associated with change. As a result, it is important that you become aware of the coming changes and how you react to them.

△

EXERCISE 10

How do You React to Change?

I would like you to take out your spiritual journal again and write your answers to the following questions:

1. How do you feel when you are forced into a situation where you are required to make a change?

2. Are you comfortable doing so?

3. Or, do you get sweaty and feel anxious about having to deal with the new change?

4. Are you excited about the opportunity change presents for you, or do you feel like hiding under a pillow while hoping it goes away?

5. Are you comfortable with change, or are you afraid to face it?

It is important that you write down your reactions as you learn more about yourself and how you find yourself reacting to change.

The reason that it is important for you to learn how you react to change is that regardless of how you respond to these questions, in the future, you will find yourself facing an increasing number of changes manifesting that you will have to deal with. This will happen because change is taking place at an unprecedented pace, that will only continue to accelerate, the closer we get to the New Age of Compassion.

My recommendation is to begin to learn to endorse it. Learn to become excited when the opportunity to change presents itself because change is going to increasingly enter your world.

The reason most of us are apprehensive about change is that we don't believe we possess the confidence in ourselves that we can handle it.

In contrast, the more you learn about yourself and how powerful you really are, the more confident you will become about facing change. Endorse it as a new exciting learning opportunity - and it will become exactly that.

As you do, you will discover that your self-confidence will expand and grow, and that you will soon realize you can handle any change that comes into your world because it has entered to assist you in your growth process. Soon, you will find yourself excited about the opportunity.

△

Most people find that change is not easy, and it isn't - for them. Many prefer to live in a state of non-change, or to experience as little change as possible, because on the surface it appears that that is the easiest thing to do.

I call this a *limbo state*. It is a state where we just try to survive, to get by, and hope that somehow, we don't attract any more fears than we already have which could hurt us even more than they already have. But those are people who don't have the new knowledge and confidence you are gaining.

While living in a limbo state may initially appear safer, we can never make progress in clearing our fears as long as our strengths, our unlimited inner being, cannot emerge. Change is required to shake us out of the limbo state.

Change situations occur to *shake us out of the lethargic state* many of us find ourselves in so we can learn to clean out the mud in our personal buckets.

Simultaneously, the process will shake up our planet so the fears of earth may begin to be dislodged.

Some people have named this the Butterfly Effect, or the principle that everything that happens, happens by design and intention, and it affects everything else, everywhere, in all of existence, since we are each a part, an integral component, of all that exists. In other words, none of us lives in a vacuum.

Because of coming to the end of the Age of Fear, we are each being faced with massive changes.

Despite the form they may take, each is contributing to the "chemicalization" process that the earth and each of us are experiencing.

This process of change is positively contributing to our spiritual growth as it is helping us learn how to better understand ourselves, our reaction to change, and how we can better integrate change into our being so we no longer need to fear it as we march forward to help ourselves, our fellow man, and earth; in its time of great need.

WE ARE LIVING IN A WORLD OF INCREASING CHANGE

"There are two basic motivating forces: fear and love. When we are afraid, we pull back from life. When we are in love, we open in all that life has to offer with passion, excitement, and acceptance."

—Jon Lennon, Beatles

In the first part of this book, we discussed the process whereby we bring our personal fears and strengths to earth so we can heal them as we make applicable changes within ourselves. Now we need to take a deeper dive into the changes taking place in our world, the reason they are taking place, and how they impact us.

That is the purpose of this chapter. The "chemicalization" process we have discussed is associated with assisting our planet prepare for the emergence of the New Age. It is similar to the ancient art of the transformation of matter (alchemy). It requires a shaking process to allow the new to emerge because change cannot occur without shaking.

While this is true with earth and its unique shaking process, the same is true, individually, with ourselves. This is why change is so important and why we need to understand it so we can adapt to it within our new spiritual context.

This chapter will also explain why the massive changes we are experiencing are taking place at this time and space, and how they fit into the overall mosaic that is taking shape, so the earth can heal itself in preparation for the New Age.

In other words, the earth is in a similar process of clearing out the fears which have been created by mankind that have, over time, immersed themselves into the earth's crust and vibration. Like us, our planet has to clear out its accumulations of fear to heal itself.

The massive changes which will occur will include much that has already been seen in miniature form: Major shifts in weather patterns such as the rise of oceans with land being dwarfed; wildfires; new drought areas; new diseases; climate change as more and more eco-system disasters take place; mental illness will become prevalent; massive economic changes will take place; and workplace upheavals will be experienced. Drinkable water will become more valuable than oil; the world of work will dramatically shift; and major changes in government, governmental policies, and world economies will take place. Shifts to spirituality will increasingly occur as members leave formalized religions.

After thousands of years of relatively little change, major changes started in the 1800s with the steam engine and cotton gin. Then, changes really began to speed up in the 1900s with the introduction of the automobile, airplane, radio, television, and space shuttle.

To illustrate how close we are coming to the new age, all we have to do is today look at the pace at which major change is taking place.

The most dramatic earth-changing occurrences in the entire history of the world have taken place in the last 25 years.

Never before have we seen or experienced so much change taking place, so fast, or so intensively.

Driven by technology, the world has been changing at warp speed. *Technological advancements have caused massive changes in how we think, live, and work.*

Since the introduction of personal computers in the mid 1990s, the world has literally been turned upside down. The scare of Y2K, and the fear of the entire world shutting down, took place only 20 years ago!

In contrast, today, Y2K is simply another antiquated concept that is not even given a second thought. Some even have to think twice before they can remember what Y2K was, or why it was so fearful to so many people – and that occurred just 21 years ago.

In 1999, cell phones were just beginning to become popular. Today, it is impossible to conceive of living without constantly updating our cell phones which have essentially become a small hand-held computer that also connects us to nearly everybody on earth. Twenty years ago, social media was not the number one topic of conversation. Newspapers, and magazines were still flourishing.

Twenty years ago, the internet was still shiny and new, and seemed to be full of exciting possibilities. A mere 20 years later, more than 4 billion people have ready access to the internet.

The majority of websites we use today weren't even a thought because websites didn't exist 20 years ago.

Today, we never think twice about not being able to smoke in restaurants, even if they were open. However, it was only 15 years ago that states began to ban smoking in restaurants.

The Hollywood film media has completely changed. Twenty years ago, Blockbusters was the place to be on the weekends so you could go in person and hope to rent the movie you wanted to watch. Shortly after that, Blockbusters started closing their stores and are now but another relic of the past like Sears and Circuit City. Today, if you want to watch a movie you can find it on Netflix, Amazon, or rent it On Demand from your television service.

More change has occurred in the workforce in the past 10 years than happened in the history of the world.

Even before the advent of COVID, 67% of the 500 largest corporations in the world were undergoing major change.

More change will cumulatively occur in the transportation industry in the next 10 years than it has since the automobile was invented 112 years ago.

Only 11% of the largest corporations in the world in 1955 still exist today.

Companies whose names we have never heard of, today employ nearly half of America's workforce (49%).

Walt Disney projects that in two years only 17% of their theme park customers will be Caucasian. This means they must change the colors and diversity of their leading characters (including their princes and princesses) in order to survive. They are aggressively in the process of doing this.

It seems like terrorism has been with us forever. However, no one lost sleep over terrorism until the Twin Towers fell 20 years ago.

Our educational systems, despite their ineptness, have been designed so graduating students can solve existing problems. However, that is no longer adequate.

Today's changes have become so rampant, and problems so pervasive, that our educational systems must not only graduate students that are trained to solve *today's problems*, but even more importantly, those graduates must be equipped to solve problems *that are not even in existence today.*

The world's population has nearly increased by one-third (30%) in the past 20 years. If that trend continues, more than one trillion people will be living by 2040. Such increases in population projections have raised all kinds of fear-filled issues including whether we can ward off mass starvation; what about hygiene, medical, and mental issues; and the rampant spread of disease caused by masses of humanity living closer than ever to one another?

The word metaphysics was found to be something strange, different, fearful, certainly not something popular 40 years ago. Positive thinking, self-development, or the recognition that we are all spiritual, was not close to being in the mainstream of thought. Today, metaphysical and spiritual beliefs have come into their own, as many people are considering spirituality or metaphysics to provide answers to the questions, they have which have not been answered by their formalized religion.

Personally, it is amazing to me as a student of Rosicrucian teachings (a metaphysical study that goes back 5,000 years to ancient Egypt) to recognize how long it has taken mankind to come to this awareness. For example, during much of the past 5,000 years it was necessary that Rosicrucian members be sworn to secrecy to avoid religious and/or government persecution.

Compare that to today where inspirational and spiritually uplifting sayings are everywhere including television, greeting cards, and posters.

Today, people are thinking differently and are considering spirituality in addition to formal religion, if not in exchange for it. This is how quickly the world has been changing its belief systems and how it is now willing to consider thinking *outside of the box* with spirituality and/or metaphysics.

The majority of these changes, as inconceivable as it may sound, have occurred during the single lifetime that you and I are living.

Then, just when we thought no other changes could so dramatically pop into our world as quickly as the aforementioned ones had happened; and we became hopeful that perhaps we could temporarily return for a few moments to our old limbo state for a moment; Covid-19 struck!

That single change, that disease alone, *has impacted every single one of us* at a speed previously considered inconceivable. It accelerated the pace of change in ways, and at speeds, which had previously been considered unimaginable.

Illustratively, within weeks, it impacted more than 190 countries, in ways that none of us could ever have envisioned in our wildest imagination. It changed nearly everything that we hold dear in terms of health, economics, and relationships. It left nothing out. Its impact was sudden, vast, and comprehensive. It seemed as if it was in all countries, everywhere, at the same time, throughout the entire planet.

That disease has *forced us to change*, whether we wanted to change or not; in how we *think*, how we *work*, and how we *live* in a way in which nothing before it ever has. *Covid has scared us to death.* It has brought the concept of fear to the forefront of our thoughts as we have had to face the potential of our own death, and of our family's death, and what that would mean. It has forced us to examine the possibility of being laid off or terminated as our employers ceased to exist. It has made us question how we could live without having money for food, rent, or medicine, if we lost our income.

It has also eroded our personal liberties. We are now told that we no longer have the right to attend church services, or to go to restaurants, to enjoy a movie at the theater, or to socialize. We are limited in our ability to travel. We cannot have family gatherings. We must wear masks. We are not allowed to see our loved ones who are in a hospital or nursing home. We must not touch other human beings and must stay at least 6-feet away from others.

Covid-19 has also given rise to increased domestic violence, suicide, and mental illness. It has forced each of us to deal with our individual agitations, anger which has been generated by the disease (remember, anger is fear under pressure), to determine how we can release the anger while our liberties are being eroded without our approval.

To some, being forced into wearing masks is akin to thousands of years where Muslim women have been forced to hide their faces without their permission, or for men and women being muzzled into being told what we can and cannot do or say. To use or not use vaccinations poses the same dilemma, as the government contemplates whether to mandate the vaccine for every man, woman, and child regardless of what they may personally think about the shots.

Despite the prevailing belief of earth in what only appears to be negative, as we have previously stated, there is always good in everything. As indicated, change is a good thing, a divine thing, because it provides us the opportunity to experience the "chemicalization" process (shaking up all of our beliefs and thought patterns so we can sort out our fearful limiting thoughts) and allow our unlimited inner self to emerge. Covid is certainly doing this for us – in spades.

$$\triangle$$

EXERCISE 11

How Are You Reacting to Covid?

Covid is affecting each of us in different ways. Accordingly, I would like you to take out your spiritual journal and write your answers to the following questions in reference to covid and the manner in which you are handling it:

1. How are you reacting to covid?

2. Are you afraid of catching this disease?

3. Have you altered your patterns of being with people out of fear that they may transmit the disease?

4. Do you stay isolated as much as possible to avoid the disease?

5. Are you afraid to get the vaccination shots?

6. Do you believe good can also occur from covid?

7. Do you believe God can be a healing energy in the vaccine shots or not?

8. Do you believe that God is more powerful than covid?

9. In what other ways are you responding to covid?

10. Do you believe you are simply "reacting" to the condition of covid; or in contrast, are you taking charge of your world to the best of your ability, in regard to how you are responding to the disease?

Remember, there is not a right or wrong answer to these questions. Rather, their main purpose is to help you gain insights into yourself, and the current process in which you respond to things.

As before, your spiritual journal is private and confidential. You are the only one who ever needs to see it.

△

Nothing is ever just good or bad. It is only to be learned from while we need that lesson. Then, we can clear the fear and the lesson never need to return. For example, while negatively impacting us in many ways, Covid has also been a blessing to many.

For example, some have found it a blessing to be able to stay at home and still be employed. Others have discovered freedom in not being forced to travel for their job while still being able to handle their business via a conference or video call. Other people have realized their skill set is increasing in demand and they have changed jobs from ones they did not like, to ones that are more satisfying. Others have turned to a cleansing process in their own homes as they have cleaned out "stuff" they had been accumulating for years, but never previously found the time to get rid of it. While others have used the extra time, they have gained to work on improving themselves mentally, emotionally, and spiritually.

Environmentally, earth has also benefited from this *time of relief*. The need for transportation to and from work decreased, people limited their travel; required work and social interactions have been significantly lessened, and the use of oil products has been reduced.

Being required to isolate ourselves from others has provided us the opportunity for self-reflection, to seriously look at who and what we are, re-examine the world in which we live, consider what it is we truly want in our individual world, and determine how spiritually unlimited do we want to become this lifetime?

There is not a better time to identify our fears and release them than now. We came to earth with the conviction we would achieve this goal in this lifetime. We now have a splendid opportunity to do so.

The planet is being filled with a powerful energy from those *spiritual teachers beyond earth and from different galaxies* to help us individually, as well as to assist the entire planet, achieve this goal. Everything is stacked in our favor. The time is now. The only thing we have to decide is whether or not we are willing to move forward and do it.

Anticipating that we do, there are two major ways to go about this process. One is to simply realize that we are all-powerful, accept that we are God in miniature form, and do it. The other way is to take a more formal approach.

Our next chapters will provide a formal mechanism that has been designed to help you implement a process to release your fears. You will be provided with three keys that had previously been hidden to help you with this cleansing process, while concurrently helping you enhance your ability to be able to achieve spiritual freedom while you are living here on earth.

You can use either approach, since either will provide you with the clean water you need to wash out and replace the old fear-laden, muddy thought patterns that have been in place and accepted by you and earth for thousands of years.

The reason that the remainder of the book will be devoted to the more formal approach to help you remove your fear is that I have found most people are more comfortable with a formal mechanism to begin with.

Then, as they become accustomed to the more structured fear clearing process, they can adjust it or custom design the mechanism to their own unique needs and personality.

Regardless of which approach you choose to use, new thought patterns, created without fear, and without the customary limitations of earth, will be necessary for the Age of Compassion and Enlightenment to emerge and manifest.

Removal of fear from our beliefs, our thought patterns, our consciousness, and our expressions, are an essential part of this change.

THREE PREVIOUSLY SECRET KEYS TO REMOVE YOUR FEARS

"If you are going to win any battle, you have to do one thing. You have to make the mind run the body. Never let the body tell the mind what to do."

—General George S. Patton

You are like the cocoon, preparing to shed the coating of fear which has prevented your true beauty, hidden inside the cocoon for so long, to emerge as the magnificent butterfly that it has always been!

In this chapter, we will discuss three previously hidden unrevealed secret keys to help us identify and release our fears so we may free the beauty of our inner magnificent butterfly. These three keys to releasing your fears have been hidden, by necessity, because you will discover as you study them, that they are in direct opposition to the teachings of formalized religion.

If these keys would have been taught and practiced in earlier years the teachers and students who possessed this knowledge would have been persecuted by the church, and likely tortured or killed, since they would have been regarded to be blasphemers.

This is the reason that at this time, when this knowledge is so badly needed by earth, that our *invisible*, nonphysical spiritual teachers, mentors from beyond earth, are bringing them to our attention.

Our spiritual teachers are like the blades on an electric fan. You can clearly see the blades when the fan is not running. However, once it is, the speed at which the energy rotates the blades, the new frequency, means that the blades are no longer visible through earth eyes.

This does not mean that the blades are no longer there; it simply means that in this new state, they have temporarily become invisible. It is the same with our *invisible* spiritual teachers and mentors. They are always with us, and they are always as real, and visible, as are the fan blades.

Our spiritual teachers have graduated from the earth experience so they are able to view earth from a different lens or prism than we are able to do since we have not yet graduated from the earth plane. It is as if they are riding in a helicopter overlooking the road from above while we are traveling on the road in an automobile. They can see the potholes or traffic jams coming up. We, in our car, can only see the roadway directly ahead.

Their singular role is to love, teach, guide, and to always be of spiritual assistance. Everyone has their own spiritual teachers.

Some are aware of this. Most are not. In the Bible, they are referred to as Angels.

The more you walk this pathway, the more articulate your invisible spiritual teachers will become in being able to communicate with you. The reason is that they operate at an extremely high level of spiritual energy while most on earth don't achieve that height of energy field consciousness. The more you grow spiritually, the more your spiritual energy will automatically increase in frequency. Nevertheless, they communicate with you in the form of dreams or thoughts that magically "seem to pop into your head" in the form of inspiration or guidance.

It is these spiritual teachers who have inspired and brought forth these Three Spiritual Keys.

The keys are incredibly powerful. They will assist you to learn to release all the fears you have constructed over the number of lifetimes you have accumulated them, since each fear you cling to prevents you from becoming right now, the *perfection which you already are.*

Every single fear, whether *supposedly* "healthy," or "unhealthy", limits you from being "all that you are". You have perfect, unlimited Divine Love within you that is seeking to express through you. But your fears act as *barriers* to this expression.

You have perfect, unlimited understanding within you, but your fears cause you to *judge* the actions of others instead of looking for the *causes* that underlie their actions.

This is the reason why we have spent time in this book helping you learn to look for *causes,* rather than only reacting to words spoken by others.

You have perfect, unlimited intelligence within you; however, your fears block your natural flow of divine inspiration. As a result, you acquire feelings of inadequacy and lack of self-confidence which cause your intelligence and inspiration to be blocked.

This is analogous to how a dam blocks the water behind it and prevents it from flowing naturally. As you remove your fears, you will discover the waters of your unlimited intelligence and inspiration once again flowing naturally and freely as they were initially created to flow by your Creative Source.

There is no longer a need for you to hold onto those kinds of blockages – all of which have been created by your own fears.

God never created these kinds of fears for you. *You did*!

Since you created the fears, you now have the opportunity, and are gaining the knowledge, of how to release them.

You may walk free without limitation. You may release all your fears in all areas and become that perfect, beautiful, unlimited spiritual, physical, mental, and emotional being who you have always been and have undoubtedly dreamt about becoming.

You may now gently, with great love and conviction, say, "I walk without fear. I am unlimited because I walk with God as my companion".

You have grown to the point where you have the opportunity to use these three incredibly powerful keys to release every single one of the limiting fears you have carried for so many years.

As you study these keys you will find that any fear you have ever had will fall under one of the three.

It will require practice, and an understanding on your part, to fully and competently use the different keys.

The more you work with them, the more proficient you will become in their use. Over time, their wisdom will become totally second-nature to you in your thinking and doing.

We initially present the three keys to clearing all your fears in their simplicity, because at first glance, they may appear to be very simplistic, and not at all profound. However, that will only be surface earth knowledge speaking as earth attempts to convince you of their lack of importance.

In contrast, I assure you that they are incredibly profound in their wisdom – although at first – I grant you, they may appear to be simple.

I can also confidently share with you that as you use the keys – you will find that they will *forever, dramatically, change how you view the world you live in, and how you interact with others going forward.*

This will also include how you find yourself interacting with yourself, and who you are becoming, as you proceed in this direction.

Because of the importance of these keys, a single chapter will be devoted to each one in order to discuss them in detail. That way we can all gain a better understanding of their scope and profound wisdom. Succinctly, the keys are as follows:

The Secret Keys To Releasing Your Fears

1. *God is Perfect, is unfathomable Wisdom, and is Eternal Love.*

2. *Man (*all of Mankind*) is a perfect soul, as are all forms of life on earth. Man is only working out an earth experience in which he attunes his earth-being to his own perfect soul.*

3. *You are perfect, spiritual and divine, and you are in the process of realizing it.*

△

EXERCISE 12

What is Your Initial Reaction to the Three Keys?

At this time, I would like you to pull out your spiritual journal and write your answers to the following questions:

- What is your honest opinion as you read these three keys?

- Do they seem to be simplistic, or profound?

- How do you react to the word "perfect"?

- Can you believe God is perfect?

- If yes, then can you also accept that mankind is perfect?

- If yes, then can you also accept that YOU are perfect?

- Can you accept that we all live in a perfect universe and learning system?

- Can you understand why they have been kept hidden and only used sparingly until now, due to the possibility of persecution?

The reason it is so important to write down your answers to these questions is so you can record your initial reaction to the keys when you first become aware of them. This way you can return to your answers in the future, reread your responses, and see for yourself how much you have learned, grown, and changed.

△

It has been my experience that students react in many different ways when they are first exposed to these previously secret keys. For example, many students initially have a negative reaction to the word "*perfect*" since they have been taught by earth that very few things, if any, are perfect.

Another common reaction is to question whether they really believe that God is *perfect*. Following discussion and a good deal of introspection, many are able to accept that God, for them, is perfect.

However, for others, it means a new review and evaluation of who and what they believe their God to be. For the vast majority, viewing God in the framework of perfection is a new and different perspective, and it takes time in order to adjust your thinking. Or, at least, it did for me.

It has also been my experience that while students tend to be much more acceptant of the *perfection of God*, they are far more reticent to accept that mankind, or especially themselves, are perfect.

The second key comes under considerable scrutiny and discussion for this reason as well as many other reasons. Some even feel the need to *fight* the knowledge associated with the second key and come up with all kinds of reasons not to accept the spiritual truth of the statement.

Examples such as Hitler, Stalin, and other mass murderers are quickly offered in order to prove that the second key is wrong. Those opinions are both quickly and strongly reinforced by others in the group. Somehow, it frequently appears that if the second key is accepted as being true; then in some way, the student must be more than what they believe they are, or that they believe, they can ever be. As a result, the second key has to be wrong.

I believe this conviction goes back to the reason so many in the world suffer from a lack of self-confidence because they are personally aware of all the errors they continually make, and believe they must punish themselves for those errors, because they are not good people. Earth teaches that each error is like a sin and must be punished. Earth also teaches that every time you make a mistake you must be punished for making that mistake

Metaphysics teaches that God does not see the errors we make because the divine knows they are simply learning lessons.

I have consistently heard these arguments over and over again when a class initially discusses the keys, together with the vehemence and energy expended in the arguments. Those arguments then bleed over into the third key, except frequently, with even more vehemence.

I have discovered that out of the three keys, the most frequently disputed is number two – perfect mankind, followed by number three – perfect me.

Somehow, students feel they must vehemently fight the teacher who attempts to teach them that we, and all of mankind, are perfect – because we inherently know that we can't be - by again, simply looking at our actions.

I also find that students are amazed at how incorrect they initially were as they begin to work with the keys and prove their truth for themselves. In addition, it has been my experience that later they tend to forget how vehemently they originally attempted to argue against the truth contained in the keys.

This is one of the main reasons why in the previous exercise I asked you to put your initial reactions in writing in your spiritual journal so you can go back in the future and see the changes you have made to yourself through your new knowledge.

Before we proceed to study each key in great depth, let me ask you to go back and once again re-read numbers two and three, except this time, read them in their entirety.

Please note that the second key clearly states that while "mankind is perfect, as is all of life on earth, man is working out an earth experience in which he attunes his earth-being to his perfect soul".

It does NOT state that man's actions and behaviors are perfect today, only that he and his soul are perfect. It emphatically states that mankind is in the *process* of growth and learning how to express his actions more and more so they are in *perfect alignment* with his perfect soul.

Most initially fail to note this distinction.

The same is true with key number three – *perfect me*. Our soul is perfect today, all of our actions are not. This is why we are in the process of working to learn and express during this lifetime on earth – how to better *align our actions and behaviors to the perfection of our soul*.

I appreciate you honestly writing down your initial reactions to these three previously hidden keys. It is a healthy discussion because it is totally foreign to what you have been programmed to believe for many years.

It truly is a paradigm shift in your mental and emotional outlook.

I know this personally because when I first learned about the keys, I had a similar reaction to what many of you have upon your first becoming aware of them. I questioned, meditated, and thought about God being described as *perfect*, because again it was a new concept to me. However, the more I thought about it the more the first key began to make total sense to me.

It was numbers two and three where I had far more reservations and had to do more soul-searching to accept the phenomenal wisdom they contained.

Today, I am totally convinced of the truth of all three keys. The reason is that I have demonstrated the truth of each statement in my personal life. I took them from a theoretical concept when I began to place them into action.

Taking these keys and metaphysical knowledge in general and putting it into action is the only way that spiritual growth can occur because if the knowledge contained in each key simply remains academic or theoretical knowledge, it will never help you come to the belief that you can release your fears and walk free in the freedom of your own strength and magnificence.

I attempt to live my life to the very best of my abilities in accordance with these three keys and the vast wisdom that each contains.

I invite you to do the same as we proceed to chapters filled with additional information devoted to each of the three keys.

GOD IS PERFECT, IS UNFATHOMABLE WISDOM, AND IS ETERNAL LOVE

"Even death is not to be feared by one who has lived wisely."

—Buddha

This is the single most important chapter in the book because it sets the foundation for everything else - what we believe our Creative Force to be. It is based on the phenomenal knowledge contained in key One.

The reason it is so important is that the attributes we define and believe our God to be, become who, and what, we believe ourselves to be.

As a builder of beautiful, large, multi-million dollar, environmentally friendly green-certified custom homes in the Washington, D.C. area, I understand the importance of building a solid foundation. Unless the new home is built on a solid concrete base, in ground that has been tested and verified to be able to sustain the weight of the new structure, the new home will crumble.

That is why this chapter is analogous to being *our foundation.*

It is a chapter about God; what God is; what God is not; how and why God created mankind, you and me; and all that exists. This chapter sets the stage for how, as children of this Creative Source, God interacts with each of us. Key number one lacks relevance or context without this background.

This chapter is devoted to helping us learn the truth about what God is, a hidden knowledge that has been known for thousands of years, but which has deliberately been kept secret from the vast majority of people due to formalized religion.

We begin by stating categorially that God is not a gigantic man on a throne somewhere in the sky that we have been taught about.

Instead, *God is Energy. God is the Energy that is in everything, and is everywhere. It is without beginning. It is without end. It is expansive and is constantly growing. It is Unlimited. It is Omnipresent, everywhere at the same time. This God Energy can be changed, but it can never be destroyed. It is Perfection in motion.*

But God is also so much more than this. God is also Unfathomable Wisdom, Eternal Love, Indescribable Goodness, Divine inspiration, Divine Health, Companionship. God is our Creative Force and our Divine Source.

God is our Parent. God created us as a Love Thought to have us join Itself in our quest for perfection.

We are the children of God, perfect, in the process of learning how to express our perfection in and through our words and actions. We are the David, the spiritual man. We are the divine being, not the Adam man, the man made of materials from earth.

We are the perfect being of a Perfect God. We have only temporarily wrapped ourselves in a human body so we could experience earth this lifetime.

Since we are the offspring of this all-loving God, we cannot be anything other than the attributes this God is - total goodness, total love, and total perfection. A loving parent who is everywhere, in all existence.

It is this God who knows each of us, who loves each of us.

It is this God who is always there when you are lonely, or feel vulnerable, or feel you need protection; a parent who will always love you no matter what errors you may or may not make; who will never leave you.

A parent from whom it is impossible to be separate - except in your own fearful thoughts.

As a youngster and into my youth, I was always scared of the man on the throne I had been taught that God was. I even considered going into the ministry of formalized religion at one time so I could be *saved by this God I so feared, instead of being potentially doomed to Hell when I died.*

It was not until I learned *what God really is* that I could release those fears and come to love this God of infinite goodness and perfection who will always look over me, protect me, inspire me, uplift me, and help me to learn how I can express all of the unlimitedness, goodness, and beauty in which it created me.

This is the God whom I have come to love – and no longer fear. I could never have come to this point of belief without my knowledge and use of metaphysics.

Some of us may be uncomfortable thinking about God in these terms since it is so foreign to what we have been taught and have accepted for so many years.

Nevertheless, even modern science is teaching us about this divine essence, but without forming using the word God. They have discovered that energy is everywhere, is in everything at the same time, is expansive, is never limited, and can never be destroyed, although it can be changed.

God is not an individual majestic being sitting on a throne somewhere in the sky waiting to judge us as we have been programmed to believe. Instead, *God, is this Energy.*

This knowledge of God that we are articulating is not new. It has been known by early mystics for thousands of years. However, it had to remain hidden, secret, because if openly taught, those espousing this wisdom would have been persecuted for balsamy; tortured, or killed by religious leaders, priests, and/or government officials in power, in order to prevent this type of heresy to spread which was against societal norms.

The knowledge that God is energy went completely against the teachings of formalized religion and would have stopped the church's revenue stream in its tracks. It also went *against the mainstream of common thought* which has been programmed into society by religion.

Instead, it was easier to keep mankind in bondage, and obedient; as long as the populace accepted an authoritarian God of vengeance; while simultaneously believing they needed to be *saved by that God*.

As long as the *Need to be Saved Belief* was in place and accepted by society, formalized religion could substantiate their control, continue to have magnificent new cathedrals built, and maintain their flow of money.

The concept of God being a single loving entity, one of great wisdom and compassion, without beginning or end, and not an angry or vindictive God, was initially espoused by Pharaoh Akhenaten in ancient Egypt approximately 5,000 years ago.

A religious reformer, he attempted to change the traditional religion of Egypt from the worship of many gods to the worship of a single god. He taught that this one God was symbolized by the sun because the sun symbolized the energy of the universe. He married Nefertiti, who in some works of art is shown standing equal next to her husband, so he was among the first to teach that males and females were equal cocreations from God.

Akhenaten is also credited by some for the creation of what is today known as the Rosicrucian Order. That organization preserved the ancient knowledge of metaphysics, founded on who and what God is as energy, as our source of being. Taught in the pyramids of Egypt in hidden format, this wisdom has been brought down through the ages to the present time.

It has been taught and perpetuated by wise, spiritually inspired teachers in many lands; while always needing to be kept hidden, under the surface, to avoid persecution, torture, and death.

It was taught by Jesus and other highly advanced spiritual leaders in parables or other forms of teachings that were publicly acceptable, but not widely understood. Unfortunately, the spiritual wisdom they taught has seldom been widely interpreted metaphysically or spiritually, until recent years.

Akhenaten was put to death by the priests who were unwilling to give up their power and authority to this radical thinking Pharaoh. The pharaoh's reforms quickly collapsed and never became mainstream. To further ensure that this would be the outcome, the priests even attempted to banish all records of Akhenaten's name to the best of their ability. His successors denounced him, and his radical concepts, and returned to the former religion of the priests and priesthood. When I was in Egypt privately visiting the museum with a professor of antiquities from the University of Cairo I personally learned how little remained of the existence of Akhenaten or his teachings.

This new concept of God visibly died, and the many fearful gods of Egypt and their admiring priests, once again prevailed.

Remember, God never hid the knowledge of Itself. This was done by mankind.

Today, we live in the time of modern science. Modern science has been enabled by recent civilizations to communicate their scientific findings publicly. They are no longer forced to communicate the church's message.

As a result, we have gained additional knowledge of the attributes of God, as we have discovered that energy is in everything that exists, animate and inanimate. Energy is the building block of all matter. All kinds of different forms are created from energy. For example, this same energy comprises the human body, animals, bricks of the house you live in, your business, your car, your phone, the forest, and the land which surrounds each of us. While its vibrations differ, dependent on the form and substance it takes, the energy is always present. It is constantly flowing.

This energy, which is everywhere, can neither be created nor destroyed, but it can be changed as it changes form and substance.

Everything in the universe is made up of this energy. It is present in different shapes and forms at any given moment in time. It is in all solar systems and all galaxies.

Modern science has dramatically expanded its knowledge of existence in recent years, and has found that earth and the other planets immediately surrounding our earth home, comprise a galaxy. In other words, the planet we are living on, earth, is only a segmental part of one solar system, within a totally unlimited universe.

Thanks to the Hubble telescope, we now know that the observable universe is estimated to contain somewhere between 200 billion to two trillion galaxies, each consisting of billions of stars, some as old as 12 billion years.

Our scientific knowledge has even increased to the point where we now have the ability to determine the proper distance between earth and the furthest edge of the observable universe, which is 46 billion light-years, making the diameter of the observable universe about 93 billion light-years, which is an *unfathomable* number.

We also know that *the observable universe is still growing*.

Years ago, when I observed the galaxies at the Chicago Planetarium, the most amazing discovery out of everything I saw or heard that day, was the statement that the universe was still *expanding*. I could accept that there was more than one galaxy in the universe in which we live. I could even accept that there are billions of galaxies because I accepted that God was and is infinite.

But what I really had difficulty getting my head wrapped around – and in a way still do - was the fact that the universe *was still growing*!

With my earth mind, my limited, finite mind, I wanted to put a nice neat bow around the existing universe, no matter how many galaxies there may be, and say *this is it – there is no more.*

But God has different ideas, because God is still growing and expanding, and can never be constrained because our Creative Source is unlimited.

Accordingly, God is continuing to procreate in all spaces and at all times.

We, as part of this infinite God, are also continuing to grow and expand. As we grow and expand, God also grows and expands. It is an ongoing process of learning and expression, growing and learning, until eventually we all return in completeness to the Godhead.

So, who and what is our God?

God is Perfect, is unfathomable Wisdom, and is Eternal Love.

God is not just energy, but is also the source of all things Good.

God is Absolute Pure Love.

God is Divine Intelligence. God is Beauty.

God is Nature.

God is Omnipresent, in all places at all times.

God is totally Unlimited.

God is Peace, Harmony, Tranquility.

God is closer than our breath.

God is everything Good that exists. God is the Source of All Good.

God is all of this and more, because it is impossible to describe God adequately with our finite earth minds or earth words.

Our God is ALL positive attributes – absolutely nothing associated with or close to any fear concepts. The extreme opposite!

This foundational wisdom of who and what God is in truth sets the stage for us to remove the fear of the erroneous concept that formalized religion has taught us for centuries about God being the bearded figure on a throne *somewhere in the sky.*

We have been taught that he, and he alone, is the judge and jury, the one who will determine our fate, even though Jesus or Mary may attempt to intercede: Who will die, who will be saved after death, and who will be doomed to live an eternity of roasting in hell. No wonder we learned to *so fear this God* we were instructed to learn about and that we had to believe in.

While in many ways this concept of God seems preposterous - it is nevertheless, the one that has been the prevailing belief of who and what God is, accepted by mankind, especially by western civilization, for many centuries.

Now think about this for a moment and try to wrap your mind around this belief system, as it is crucially important in recognizing how we have come to think and act in the manner in which we have, by and through our own fears of God.

Can you see how all of these concepts of God are *fear-based?*

In other words, formalized religion has taught us that despite our being the children of God, we are offspring who *must* be subservient; *powerless* to think or function on our own; weak; *judged* on whether we *sin* or not and how much; and that we must be saved by something more powerful than we are, which can only be found outside of ourselves.

We have been taught that judgment is a good thing and not something bad.

Power over others is fine as long as we are the ones in the power position.

Doing something sinful is okay as long as it is forgiven by the church or a special tithe is paid.

Criticizing a non-church goer is okay.

Giving to the church is always a good thing whether it is in the form of money or servitude.

Gaining wealth for ourselves (a form of independence) is not good, since we have been taught how difficult it is for a rich man to get into heaven.

These are all examples of the type of fears we have allowed others *to stamp on our foreheads and embed in our consciousness.*

The fearful perceptions of God that have been programmed into us, and that *we* have accepted, have become a *Blanket of Fear that* each of us has woven.

As the weavers of this cloth, we have tightly wrapped the Blanket of Fear, the fabric of limitation, around ourselves. We have worn it and have taken comfort in it, since it has been woven with the belief of what we had been taught by formalized religion, which has in turn been continually reinforced by societal norms.

It has become a part of the vibrational fabric of fear which surrounds the planet and our underlying, prevailing thought patterns – all of which have been based *on false teachings* regarding *who and what God is.*

In contrast, today, based on our new truth, our new knowledge of God – being *Perfect, Unfathomable Wisdom, and Eternal Love* - the foundation has been laid as an underpinning to the first key.

The next chapter, designed to expand our knowledge of the second key, builds on this new foundational understanding and knowledge of God.

MAN IS A PERFECT SOUL, AS ARE ALL FORMS OF LIFE ON EARTH. MAN IS ONLY WORKING OUT AN EARTH EXPERIENCE IN WHICH HE ATTUNES HIS EARTH-BEING TO HIS OWN PERFECT SOUL

"I'm not afraid of storms, for I'm learning how to sail my ship."

—Louisa May Alcott

The previous chapter used the first key to establish the foundation for all that God is.

The purpose of this chapter is to look at the second key, perfect mankind, and recognize who and what *man* is, within the context of this new knowledge of God. The reader also needs to be aware that when we are using the word *man, or mankind*, we are referring to all human beings who inhabit the planet. We do so without reference to sex, nationality, or race.

Based upon this new awareness - that God *is Perfect*, is *unfathomable Wisdom*, and is *Eternal Love* - requires that we first look at *how* we were created and came into existence so we can better understand *who* we are.

God created man through an all-knowing Love Thought. As simple, or as profound as that. Nothing more and nothing less.

This means that God is our parent, our Creative Force. In this manner, God has created each of us – mankind - from the same precise substance that God is: *Divine Energy, Eternal love, Intelligence of the Universe, Perfection*.

Therefore, man has been conceived –created by God –*Perfect by Conception, although not yet by realization!*

The same is true with all forms of life on earth: Animals, plants, mountains.

I personally like to compare God to an ocean. Perhaps the reason I enjoy the analogy of God being the ocean is that Susan and I live part of the year in the Caribbean and are able to enjoy being in the ocean nearly every day. It is incredibly serene and peaceful to be on the beach overlooking the ocean while the clouds gently float by and the trade winds provide a gentle cooling breeze.

The beach we spend time on is in the Turks and Caicos and it is rated the number one beach destination in the world. The reason for the ranking is that it has a wide beach with fantastically soft white sand coupled with magnificent waters that are clearly visible to great depths.

The waters are stunning and have different layers of color. For example, the closest waters to the beach are a light blue; the next layer out from the beach is a brilliant turquoise; the layer further out is a darker blue. Collectively, as the water colors blend together, they are magnificent and to me truly reflect the beauty of my God. I always feel as if I am in the presence of God whenever I am on this beach.

This is the reason why, to me, symbolically, God is the water in the ocean with all of its magnificence, blended colors, cleanliness, power, and abundance of life. I can see God so clearly being the ocean when I am in the ocean: Gigantic, powerful, infinite, non-ending, constantly in motion.

While these waters represent God, to me, they also represent man, because while God *is the ocean*, we, as children of God, are the *drops of water* that collectively *form* the ocean.

Like a droplet of water, we are *not, and can never be all* that God is. However, we *are everything* that God is, in terms of *all* the same *elements that God is,* has ever been, and will be – the only difference being that we are in *miniature form.*

This means that we possess *all* of the attributes of our Creative Source. In other words, we have been *conceived and born with the same DNA as God.* We cannot get away from it even if we try, since our DNA was gifted to each of us at our conception by God.

The secret of this chapter, is that mankind and all forms of life on earth have been endowed by the DNA of our All-Loving Creative Source of Goodness. This means that when we envision God as being *Eternal Love,* we are gifted with *Eternal Love.* When we acknowledge that God represents the totality of the ocean and that man represents each of the drops of water in the ocean, we are acknowledging that God is *Perfection,* which means that as the children of God we are also perfect. It is in our DNA.

As I shared earlier, it is always interesting to me that whenever I share this knowledge in a lecture or workshop, participants are much more ready to accept *God being perfect*, than they are to accept that *mankind is also perfect*. Some even become belligerent, adamant that they are not, and cannot, be perfect!

Again, I am always fascinated by this reaction because it strongly reinforces our tendency to undervalue ourselves in comparison to someone or something else, while quickly pointing out our fallacies, and concurrently fighting the concept of man's perfection. While fascinating, the reason it is not surprising is that we have been *trained* to believe these false things about ourselves.

I readily agree that mankind is not perfect, by expression, today. But the spiritual truth remains we have been *created perfect* by conception, by our DNA. That is accurate and indisputable. The reason we are *on earth and in this incarnation is to learn how to express* more and more of the gift of perfection we were given at conception.

I always find it fascinating that Hitler is consistently who the majority of people associate with *evil*, not Stalin, who killed even more people than Hitler; or Mao who killed more people than Hitler and Stalin combined; or other dictators who have been responsible for killing millions of people.

Because of the constancy of the Hitler question, we asked our spiritual teachers from beyond earth to further clarify the second key. They reiterated that the second key means that man is perfect by conception – by design - *not yet by expression*.

They continued by adding that man is like an infant who is just in the process of learning how to walk on earth while attempting to express the perfection in which they were created. The purpose of the earth is to be a teacher so mankind can learn to collectively express their gifts to the fullest of their abilities while doing so without fear.

They readily acknowledged that man makes many mistakes while learning to express their perfection. For example, many try to deny that man is perfect because it is easier to blame our imperfections on others, rather than to accept responsibility for our own actions. Next, they try to pretend that God is not perfect, so they in turn could not be perfect. Finally, they tend to act out all kinds of ill-advised behaviors that *prove* they are not perfect.

However, regardless of the number of errors committed and the time it may take, mankind will eventually come to the realization that they are *perfect by conception from God*, and they *will* complete their spiritual journey to express their individual perfection – in action and in deed.

Our invisible teachers concluded by sharing that Hitler did indeed cause incredible pain and suffering. However, he, like all of mankind, is in the process of learning how to express the perfection of his creation in his actions. Because of his earth actions in his past life, he has already reincarnated back into earth to create the opportunity for new learnings which is much quicker than the normal cycle.

For example, during his current incarnation, he is one of Mother Theresa's Nuns, working with the worse of the worse, the dirtiest of the dirtiest, the poorest of the poorest, the most filthy of the filthy, in the most unimaginable, dire, conditions. In this filthy environment, he is in the process of *beginning to learn* the lesson of compassion.

Certainly, few of us believe that Hitler, nor mankind, is expressing to the fullest their perfection, or their abilities at the present time. Despite this, it does not detract from the fact that each of us, in one form or other, is in the *process of learning how* to express the perfection in which we were created, regardless of whether we may be consciously aware of it or not while being in earth this time.

This is where the *distinction* lies: Being *Perfec*t *by design, by conception*, is one thing. Having the capability to express it, at all times, in all of our thoughts and actions, is something *totally different*.

This is why earth and other places of living exist. Man is on a quest, a journey, which will take as long as mankind requires, to not only discover and accept that he is perfect, but also to learn how to express that perfection, continuously, in every one of his thoughts, and in every one of his actions.

Few have reached the state of being able to fully express their perfection, even though we have had splendid spiritual teachers help us including Jesus, Buddha, and Confucius.

It is why God gave each of us pencils with erasers when our Creative Force set every single member of the human race on our journey to discover and experience the freedom of living without fear.

Man is on earth, during this time, in order to live a life different than any he has ever previously experienced.

His role in this life is to learn more about his perfection, and to learn more about expressing that perfection in his everyday thoughts, beliefs, and actions.

He can increasingly do this by releasing more and more of the fear he has carried for so long.

As a part of mankind, we are all in the process of experimenting and learning. All make mistakes and will become wiser because of the mistakes we have made. When we do, hopefully, we will not repeatedly make the same mistakes over and over again.

This is the *purpose of life*, whether it is expressed here on earth, or on another planet, or in a different galaxy: To grow spiritually, to share with others, and to learn to continually express more and more of the perfection in which God conceived mankind, in our every thought, action, and deed.

YOU ARE PERFECT, SPIRITUAL AND DIVINE; AND YOU ARE IN THE PROCESS OF REALIZING IT

"One of the greatest discoveries a man makes, one of the great surprises, is to find he can do what he was afraid he couldn't do."

—Henry Ford

The previous chapter laid our foundation for the second key's knowledge that mankind is perfect by conception and design, although not yet, by realization or expression.

This chapter is designed to help us look at ourselves within our new knowledge of God and mankind, as an individual creation of God, so we may recognize the inner beauty, the unlimitedness, of who and what each of us is as an individual.

Based upon the new awareness that God *is Perfect, unfathomable Wisdom* and *Eternal Love*, we need to recognize the phenomenal impact this new knowledge can have on us.

Essentially, it means that *every single person*, by conception, is a unique and divine spark of life that has been brought into existence by our Creative Source.

Therefore, our persona, our inner being, our consciousness, our existence, *are perfect, spiritual and divine* –despite our only being in the early stage of learning about it, and am only beginning to express it.

No longer do we need to accept, as taught by formalized religion, that we are sinners, mistake-prone, and bound for hell as punishment for our evil deeds. Instead, we can put those false teachings behind us and begin to concentrate our attention on clearing fear and becoming the inner magnificence we have been created to be.

This requires a momentary leap in faith on our part since we need to at least *temporarily accept*, to the best of our ability, that God is our parent and our Creative Force. It requires we recognize that God has created everyone - you and me - from the *identical substance* of energy that God is – *Eternal love, Divine Intelligence, Personal Power, Self-confidence.*

I know that for many of you this is a *total paradigm shift* in your thinking, and in your thought patterns. It may even initially be shocking.

If it is, it would not be surprising since this new knowledge is the absolute opposite of what we have been taught about God, mankind, and ourselves, for whatever number of years we have lived.

However, in order to begin to apply this incredibly new, but ancient wisdom, it is necessary that we begin to at least preliminarily accept it; and then use and apply this new knowledge, so we can confirm its truth and applicability for ourselves.

If we don't, it will simply be a new and interesting theory. A fascinating academic concept. One without relevance, because it won't have been practiced, or proven by ourselves.

To do this requires that we step back for a moment and look at the process of how we were born. When we do, we will see how quickly we gave up the unlimited spiritual being we knew ourselves to be while we were *beyond earth,* when we entered this earth plane, as a baby.

Look at any newborn child. Everyone loves them even though it seems like all they do is cry, eat, and sleep. They cry a lot. And they are fed a lot.

Now, think more deeply about the reaction that takes place in response to the baby's crying. The baby is helpless and it cries. As a result, it is fed.

Now, picture *yourself* as *being that baby* because you *were that baby* at one time. The moment you cried, your parents instantly reacted and quickly fed and comforted you – regardless of whether it was in daylight hours or the middle of the night. Your cries were always met with responsiveness and food, without reservation, regardless of whether your parents were considered by society to be functional or dysfunctional people.

This behavior pattern was essential - because if you had not been fed on a regular basis - you would have died.

Now, take another look at all the power you had over your parents as an infant!

Even though you were in an infant body, you still had the remembrance from your *beyond earth experience* that you were an unlimited spiritual being. You knew your cries would elicit immediate attention because of the power you had within. And, they did!

Now, that is what we call *Personal God Power*!

God's power is gentle and loving, in contrast to earth power, which is harsh and controlling.

In addition to being born in perfection, you were also born with incredible God Power, the knowledge that you were a spiritual being who was temporarily residing in an earth body so you could learn to express the gifts God had given you. For example, you knew when you cried, you would instantly be fed. This is the Spiritual Law "Ask and ye shall receive", in action.

In other words, as a baby, you had *God Power* over your world. You accepted it and you used it. You knew you were loved by your parents and you knew if you cried, which was your way of alerting your parents to the fact that you were hungry, you would be fed. You believed it and your words manifested themselves into what you had requested, which was food.

However, as you grew, it was not as necessary that you be fed as immediately or as frequently as when you were a baby. As a result, sometimes when you cried, you were not immediately fed. The more this happened, the more you gradually learned that your parents were in control of the *timing* of your well-being. You continued to use your God Power, and your cries *continued to be* greeted with food, but not with the same urgency.

Simultaneously, you began to learn about *earth fears*. If you cried, and if your parents did not respond right away with food, would that mean that they might, possibly, *forget*, that you needed to be fed?

What would happen to you if they did forget?

You also learned to accept that your parents and other authority figures *had more power over you than your real God* – because *they* could decide *when* to feed you, when to *scold* you, when to *compliment* you, and when to love you. You also learned *they had to be obeyed*. As a result, through this process of earth learning, you learned it was necessary to give up your God Power, and in its place, accept the power of earth.

The older you became; the more authority figures came into your world and the more God Power, you gave them. Authority figures included your siblings, grandparents, cousins, teachers, ministers, policemen, and bosses. Each demanded something from you regardless of whether it was simply love, or a form of obedience. Each began to criticize and correct you as you grew. Each punished you when you did something wrong.

Through this process you began to learn the importance of punishment, and how you couldn't be loved unless you were punished first.

For example, if you broke something, you were punished, and then loved afterward. If you ran across the street and nearly got hit by a car, your mom would grab you, spank you out of her fear, and then hug and love you, because she was so relieved you were okay.

But to a child's mind you had done something wrong, gotten punished, and then you were loved. So, it became a learned pattern.

Because you were constantly being corrected and punished by your authority figures, even by your siblings, you also learned that you were *defective.* Again, to the child's mind, if you had not been defective, you wouldn't have always had to be corrected. So, you accepted the belief you were far less than perfect.

Patterns like these were confusing because you knew as a spiritual being they did not make sense. Nevertheless, the more those learnings were constantly reinforced, the more they became your reality. As a result, your fears began to manifest and grow.

The more you gave up your personal strength and freedom, which you possessed when you first came to earth, the more fears you began to accumulate which replaced the original belief you had in yourself. As a result, you gave up more and more of your God Power and your loving, unlimited, spiritual self.

As your fears grew, you lost more and more of your self-confidence and self-esteem. Decisions became far more difficult than they were as a baby when the only decision you had to make was to cry when you were hungry.

Making a decision now meant that you had to word it correctly, and that you had to properly say your *please and thank you's,* or you might not get what you needed, or wanted. Again, earth reinforced that *it,* and its authority figures were in charge, not your God Power.

Also remember, that to a child, all authority figures were giants. Therefore, they became the Gods that the child was to worship.

As a result, you learned to pass decision-making responsibilities to your authority figures. Since they were older, and apparently wiser than you were, you figured they must also be able to make better decisions.

You also learned over time that your *authority figures* would be more inclined, or motivated, to do what you wanted them to do if you obeyed the suggestions *they made,* rather than listening to your own vision. It was in this manner that you began to learn how to manipulate while you concurrently learned you could not make your own decisions.

The more you practiced the ways of earth, the more you became limited, which was what earth was teaching you; and the more you accepted limitation, the more you lost your self-esteem and self-confidence.

The process continued as priests and ministers gave you their fearful concepts of God. As a child, you learned that your role was to accept and obey, and your mind became increasingly filled with the fears you were taught about religion's vengeful and judgmental God; a God who detested wealth except that which was given to the church; and that man was just an inferior creature that sinned continuously.

The same holds true with your teachers who provided you with your formal education. Your parents, grandparents, and relatives continually reinforced that your teachers and ministers were wise and had to be obeyed. This might have been fine if your teachers had taught that you should learn to think for yourself, use your own abilities, and make decisions on your own; but seldom was that their approach.

Instead, the learnings you were taught focused on accepting without question that you should never think *out of the box,* and that you were *always* to obey authority figures.

The more strength and power you *gave* your teachers, the greater their influence became, which should not be surprising. That influence was actually studied by Rosenthal and Jacobsen in 1968. They discovered that when positive results were expected by teachers from their students, those expectations influenced positive performance. In contrast, when the teacher espoused and expected negative performance, it caused negative results from their students.

This psychological phenomenon became known as the Pygmalion Effect. When we expect certain behaviors from others, there is a high probability that that expected behavior will occur. The Pygmalion Effect takes place every day.

Our parents influence our behavior as they exert their expectations regardless of whether that is positively or negatively presented. Our ministers influence our thinking and actions as they instruct us regarding how we have to behave. Bosses and other authority figures continually influence our behavior as they lay out their instructions and our expected responses.

Sometimes it seems like everybody else has more influence on and over your behavior and your performance than you do. And, to a large degree this is true – but it is only because you have allowed it to become true.

The same holds true with your thoughts, since your dominant thoughts are what manifest in your world.

The power of the Pygmalion Effect, as I shared earlier, certainly had a great influence on me when I was in high school when my homeroom teacher gave an assignment that each of us was to discuss what we planned to do after graduation. When it came to my turn, I responded that I planned to go to college. My teacher snorted under his breath, and said, "Dick, you need to rethink that because you are not smart enough to go to college!"

I was shocked, stunned, and *embarrassed* in front of my classmates. His comments had certainly negatively impacted me.

While I had never thought of myself as being the most brilliant scholar, I certainly had not considered myself to be dumb, or at least not smart enough to go to college even though I was the first in my family to ever do so!

This negative perception stayed with me for many, many years; and still periodically attempts to "pop up" into my conscious as a fear which needs to be cleared at an even deeper level.

Illustratively, even though I did earn an undergraduate degree, two master's degrees, an MBA, a Ph.D., a metaphysical ministerial degree, and numerous executive degrees in such varied disciplines as economics, organizational behavior, value engineering, marketing, and real estate, I always had the tendency to question my own intelligence and perceived that somehow, I had *always fooled my professors and bosses.*

I use this example because I believe it vividly illustrates how we, as individuals, are willing to give up our personal power, our God Power, our intelligence, and our own self-confidence to authority figures who appear to know more than we do, but in retrospect likely don't even know what they are talking about – especially when they make false, negative proclamations, like my former teacher did.

I believe it also clearly illustrates how in my individual situation, I had allowed my authority figure's comments, for years, to instill fear while negatively eroding my personal self-worth and confidence.

This example also serves to illustrate that no matter how many degrees a person may earn, if their base belief remains in place that they are not very intelligent, they will steadfastly hold on to *that false belief* instead of changing it to accept the reality that if they were not intelligent, they never would have earned those degrees. In other words, as a wise teacher once told me, you cannot *fool that many people, all of the time.*

The power lies in what YOU believe about yourself. If you believe you are smart, and operate that way, you will be. If you believe you are not intelligent, you will find ways to reinforce that lack of belief in yourself.

The Spiritual Law is that what you believe about yourself is what you will express. This is why I always say if you don't like something about yourself, then change it. If you don't, you will continue to manifest who you were before the change. It is as simple, or as profound as that.

The manner in which fear teaches us to give up our power, our self-confidence, our self-value, is insidious, and it takes place over time. The more we give up, release, or forget the *beyond-earth knowledge of our spiritual self,* and our spiritual gifts, the more we fill our consciousness with fear.

God gave each of us an incredible gift, our brain, at the time of our conception. Our brain's capacity is nearly as incredible as God Itself. Illustratively, our brain is capable of processing up to 30 billion bits of information per second.

Your brain boasts the equivalent of 6,000 miles of wiring and cabling. Typically, the human nervous system contains at least 50 billion neurons which are nerve cells designed to conduct impulses. While the neurons act independently, they also communicate with other neurons through an amazing network of more than 100,000 miles of nerve fibers.

The power of our brains to process information is staggering and demonstrates how truly *unlimited* we actually are. It is even more amazing when you consider that a computer – even the fastest computer – can only make connections one at a time. By contrast, a reaction in one neuron in our brain can spread to hundreds of thousands of other neurons in a span of fewer than 20 milliseconds. That is about 10 times less time than it takes to blink your eyes.

While a neuron takes a million times longer to send a signal than a typical computer switch, the brain can still recognize a familiar face in less than a second. It is able to achieve this speed because, unlike the computer, all of its billions of neurons can simultaneously attack a problem.

Unfortunately, despite all of the incredible intellectual capacity we have been born with, we have allowed our many fears to enter our consciousness. We have allowed them to diminish our self-belief and the confidence that we can accomplish anything we put our mind to, or that we desire.

Since our subconscious can only produce what we consciously believe –that is what it does. As a result, the incredible power which we possess, and which has always been at our disposal since our divine conception, is shut down and goes unused.

We have allowed our fears to convince us that we are *limited* – thus *we have become limited*– despite all of the capabilities innate within each one of us as an individual.

Based on this new knowledge, we need to begin to reexamine the false earth assumptions we have created - and accepted - through our fears.

It is earth that has taught us to believe that we are *not* powerful, *and certainly, could not be unlimited*.

The reason is that each of us, as individuals, is intimately aware of all the defects and limitations we have; know that we frequently *lack* self-confidence; under-value ourselves; have difficulty making decisions on our own; and when we do make a decision, immediately begin to second-guess our initial decision.

We believe we are lesser than others; certainly, do not believe we are perfect; and instead believe we are not even very intelligent much of the time; let alone being smart. We accept and believe in our non-intelligence, despite the fact that we have more than 50 billion neurons available at our disposal, which, if effectively utilized, would readily verify our intelligence.

We have been taught to believe that our lives are limited, and we have accepted that earth belief to be our belief.

As a result, because our subconscious mind can only manifest our predominate thoughts, we limit the power we believe our God to be, and ourselves, because it is those limiting and less than perfect thoughts that must manifest based on our beliefs.

The reality is that all of *those limiting beliefs from earth are completely false*.

Since our Creative Source created each of us as a love thought, we are the undisputed offspring of our God – perfect, with unfathomable wisdom, universal God power, self-confidence and self-esteem. Each one of us is *perfect, spiritual and divine*, despite the fact that we are just in the process of realizing and expressing these gifts.

God has created each of us as a miniature God. We become that miniature God in and for our world. This is the world that we live in daily, and create daily.

We have created the miniature world we live in with our thoughts. Nothing requires that we accept fear; nor do we need to accept any limitations in our world despite earth's attempts to constantly teach us that we are limited.

The moment we choose to accept that we are not limited, as the earth has attempted to teach us, we can revert back to our original state of unlimitedness.

Like a muscle that has atrophied, all it will take is practice, or rehabilitation, a new way of thinking and doing, to regain the ability to again express our unlimitedness.

As we do, we will again be using the personal God Power and the ability to fully express our spiritual being, our Spiritual David, instead of our earth man.

The fact that we have not done so, simply means that when we were children we believed and behaved like children, and we did childish things.

The spiritual truth is that each of us is perfect, spiritual and divine. We are also just in the process of realizing it and beginning to put our perfection into practice.

Now that we are in the process of becoming spiritual adults, based on the new knowledge we are acquiring, we have the opportunity to readjust and change our beliefs and thoughts while accepting that *we are perfect, we are spiritual, and we are divine.* When we do, we can express and act accordingly.

The sooner we recognize this spiritual truth, the sooner we can accept our new vision and wisdom; and produce new results from our positive, loving, and unlimited thoughts in our daily actions; in contrast to the limiting ones that we used to express.

Whether we choose to take a direct path up the top of the mountain, or take indirect, alternate paths and detours, is a decision each of us has to make; because the spiritual reality is that regardless of which road we choose, each of us, as individuals, together with all of mankind; will eventually get to the top of the spiritual mountain.

Once we are at that highest point, each of us will, as individuals, come to the realization that we have been conceived by our Creative Source perfect, spiritual and divine; we will express this wisdom in *all of our thoughts and in all of our actions* because we will have completed our individual journeys; and we will have once again returned to our God-Head, our Creator; expressing the individualized perfection in which we were originally created.

USE THE KEYS TO RELEASE YOUR FEARS

"Fear keeps us focused on the past or worried about the future. If we can acknowledge our fear, we can realize that right now, we are okay. Right now, today, we are alive, and our bodies are working marvelously. Our eyes can still see the beautiful sky. Our ears can still hear the voices of our loved ones."

—Thich Nhat Hanh

Since we have gained an understanding of the three keys, we can now begin to place individual fears under the appropriate one so we can analyze each of our fears, heal them, and reclaim the space they had previously occupied within our consciousness. Those fears will then lose the legitimacy they previously held. In turn, the vibrational layer of fear we have forced ourselves to think and function through will be minimized, and eventually cease to exist, because we will have given ourselves the gift of freedom to allow our unlimitedness to flow unimpeded.

In other words, your fears will be vanquished forever. Their toxicity will cease. Their stranglehold, mentally and emotionally, will stop.

Since Nature abhors a vacuum, you will have a newly emptied space within your consciousness that you can fill with divine love. The reason that love is recommended as the replacement is that love energy will allow you to manifest and bring forth the good in your world in whatever substance or form you wish it to manifest regardless of whether that be prosperity, health, relationships, self-confidence, or all.

The purpose of this chapter is to begin to work this process, together, so you can regain your own God Power and strength. During future chapters, we will use examples of common fears in an effort to illustrate and teach the process of fear clearing under each key.

There are many different fear clearing methods that can be used to effectively cleanse the fears you have carried for so many years. The reason for different approaches is because each of us is different and we are unique individuals in how we approach things, plus it is important we are able to maintain as much comfortability in our individual process of releasing fear as possible.

The fear clearing process also needs to be *joyful* since we are reclaiming the self-confidence and power God gave us at birth. *Joy* means that we are on our spiritual path, we know it, and we rejoice in that knowledge.

Some may want to take their identified fear into their meditation to release it using the keys during that prayerful time. Others may find it more comfortable to keep a personal and confidential journal and write down each of their identified fears, followed by journaling how to release them using the keys. Some people may want to use a spreadsheet to methodically keep track of their work. Still, others may find additional methods of implementing the fear clearing process through their use of the keys.

No individual process is right or wrong. Rather, the correct process is the one that works for you and, most importantly, is the one that you practice.

Again, there is no right or wrong way. The only important thing is that you use the method you are most comfortable using and that you continue its use. If you begin using one approach, and later find it easier or more effective to transition to another, that is perfectly acceptable and understandable.

The important thing is to do the work to release your fears. Otherwise, it will not happen, it will remain an academic process, and you will continue to keep yourself in emotional and mental bondage, personal slavery, while continuing the limitations you have created which are blocking your goodness from being expressed.

EXERCISE 13

Take One of Your Fears and Analyze it

I ask that you now take out your spiritual journal and prepare to do the following: First, pick out one of your favorite fears. Please write it down in your journal. Then re-read and re-examine the three keys. Next, having the three in front of you please write your answers to the following questions:

1. Which of the three seems to be the most logical to help you release the fear you have selected"?

2. Then, ask yourself "If you were to select one of the three keys to write your fear under, which one would it be?"

Please write your answers in your journal because this will be the preparatory stage to help you begin the process to heal all of your fears.

EXERCISE 14

If You Select Key One – Perfect God

Once you determine the key that most fits the fear you have selected, confirm its applicability by asking yourself the following questions from key one:

1. Do you believe God will punish you if and when you make mistakes or errors?

2. Do you believe God is judgmental, and if you have sinned, will send you to hell?

3. Do you believe God knows all the bad things you have done?

4. Do you have the fear you have selected because you believe that God is something other than good?

5. Do you believe God is separate from you?

6. Do you believe that God gets angry at you when you make a mistake?

7. Do you believe God walks in one direction while you walk in a totally separate direction?

These are examples of the types of questions that are important to ask yourself as you implement this process. Decide under which key you should place your fear, and answer the questions under that fear as part of your self-analysis, so you can work on the fear and heal it.

These are in-depth questions rather than surface ones such as, "What is God? (Key One); What is man? (Key Two) What am I" (Key Three). It is important that you don't stop with surface questions. The power of this process is to continue to analyze and ask yourself in-depth questions so you can truly begin to dislodge the fears you have carried.

You will also discover that the more you work on this process, the more in-depth questions you will be inspired to develop for yourself. As you do, I suggest that you add them to this list in your spiritual journal since they are important to help you heal your fear.

The reason we are using in-depth questions is that when we choose to work to clear our fears, we are doing in-depth work within our conscious and subconscious minds. Deep analysis requires in-depth questions and self-examination. Surface questions will not suffice or get the job done.

As you examine the fear you have preliminarily chosen, compare it against the questions related to each key. In order to do this, you will need to re-read the Exercise questions related to each key in this chapter. When you finish comparing your fear to the questions under each key, you will then be able to determine which key has the kind of questions that best applies to the fear you have chosen. This process will allow you to take the preliminary decision you made for a key selection, and allow you to confirm it, or reject it and select a new key.

This will then become the key you will choose to work your fear which will grant you the ability to release the negative energy from it so you can heal it.

Also, be aware, that some fears will seem to be applicable to more than one key. When that happens, select the key that seems to be the predominant one. There will always be one key that is predominant, while another may be applicable, but secondary.

EXERCISE 15

If You Select Key Two – Perfect Man

Then ask yourself questions such as these:

1. Does mankind, humanity, believe there is a God of good?

2. Does mankind desire to do things that are good?

3. Does mankind feel good about themselves when they do things that they instinctively know are not good for others?

4. Does mankind believe that there is prosperity available for everyone?

5. Does mankind believe there is only so much, or only a limited amount of prosperity to go around, and therefore man has to ensure he gets his, first?

6. Does mankind desire to do things that are less than perfect?

Does mankind think if he believes in a God of good, then that would mean that mankind is good, because man would not seek goodness if he did not correspond to this good?

EXERCISE 16

If You Select Key Three – Perfect Me

Then ask yourself questions such as the following ones:

1. Do you, as an individual, believe that God is good, and nothing but goodness; and therefore, you are also good?

2. Even if others think you are good, do _you_ believe you are?

3. Do you purposely separate yourself from God through your procrastination, laziness, anger, and need to be accepted by others?

4. Do you believe that God is a God of Prosperity, and has provided for unlimited prosperity to go around for everyone, including you?

5. Do you believe that God is a God of Health, and has gifted you with outstanding health?

6. Or do you believe you are defective and that others are more powerful than you?

7. Do you believe you need to be punished when you make a mistake?

8. Do you believe that God is Perfect; Therefore, you are also perfect by design, even though not yet by expression?

$$\triangle$$

As you continue this process to heal your fears, additional questions for each of the keys will come to your aware conscious mind. You should write them in your spiritual journal and then work them under the appropriate key.

In the following pages, we will devote one chapter to each key by analyzing in-depth how it can be used to clear your fears. We will select a fear common to each of us and use questions from the exercises about it. Part of the process will include the reason why that fear was placed under the specific key that it was.

Each chapter has been planned as an example for you to learn from, so in the future, you can effectively use the keys by yourself to help you release each fear you choose to analyze and heal.

I have chosen three fears to work on and to heal. They are (1) Fear of Death (2) Fear of Authority, and (3) Fear of Health.

The reason I chose to use these three specific fears is that they have *consistently* been identified by workshop participants to be among their top three fears, regardless of whether the workshops were conducted in the United States, Mexico, or overseas.

We placed the Fear of Death under Key One – Perfect God - because we associate God with Death, and fear what happens to us after we die.

We placed the Fear of Authority Figures under Key Two – Perfect Mankind - because authority figures are always outside of ourselves such as parents, teachers, priests/clergy, and relatives, and are always part of mankind, or humanity, in general.

We placed the Fear of Health under Key Three – Perfect Me – because the belief or lack of belief in abundant health comes from within each of us as individuals, and then in turn, manifests into our physical bodies.

USING KEY NUMBER ONE

"People living deeply have no fear of death." —Anais Nin

We start our fear clearing process by selecting one of the most common fears people have – *Death*. We will dissect what we have come to believe about death so in turn we can remove our fear of it.

All of us know that death is imminent, and will eventually happen to each of us while we are on earth since death is a part of life. However, that does not make the fear of death any less real or scary. Therefore, it is a perfect fear to use as an example to learn how to examine and heal all of our fears.

I have diligently worked on myself to clear this specific fear since the subject of death, and the fear of what happens to us when we die, is common-place and is integrally linked to what our belief in God is; especially at the time of our passing. This is why key number one was chosen to heal this fear.

Also, remember, you will create what you believe. So, if you believe in a place called hell, and you believe you deserve to go to hell, then that is what you will design, or create, and choose to live in until you decide it is time to change your belief; and therefore, change your experience. The moment you do, hell will no longer exist for you and you will be freed of that experience.

I know there are people who say they don't believe in God, or certainly don't believe in a God who sits on a throne somewhere in the sky.

While I understand the lack of belief in a God sitting on a throne, it is always fascinating to me that the closer one comes to their own death; the more everyone that I know, regardless of their earlier thinking patterns about God, especially those who previously failed to believe in God; want to discuss and learn more and more about God.

I know, on a personal basis, I very much used to have a heavy-duty fear of God and of death until I cleared that fear from my consciousness.

The First Step

The first step in the fear clearing process is to select the fear and place it under the applicable key. This has already been done with this Key and the subject of death.

The Second Step

Next, it is important to think about and answer the questions associated with the first key to start your analysis of an in-depth understanding of what you do and do not believe about God, death, and your related fear about it.

The Third Step

After you do that, you next need to start writing a narrative in your spiritual journal regarding your beliefs and fears about death.

The questions associated with this key were designed to help "*soften you up*" so the vulnerability of your fears can begin to *come to the surface,* and be exposed to the light of spiritual truth. This is important, because as you begin to put your thoughts in writing, you will find you will be inspired to write more and more and more.

Gradually, over time, the process will become more and more natural and you will find yourself writing and revealing more and more about the fear(s) that you had previously kept hidden.

This will happen because when you write, it is as if *you* are no longer in charge of filtering your thoughts. Instead, it is like you are simply becoming a scribe, or a stenographer, who is putting words on paper that are coming unfiltered from your subconscious mind.

Don't judge them. Don't worry about the grammar or spelling. Just continue with the flow. Keep on writing as the words come to you. Your non-judgment is critically important in this process. In other words, just get your words on paper. That is the important thing.

Write as much as you are inspired to write, and believe me, you will be inspired to write more and more and more, as your mind fills with what to put on paper. The reason is that this will likely be the first time your consciousness has had the opportunity to begin to dump its fearful content so it can begin the healing process.

Later, you can come back and read what you have written. By tackling your fear in this manner, you are *no longer reacting to it.* Reaction infers that you are not in charge. Instead, you are simply a puppet being jerked around by external events that you simply react to and cannot control. Now, with the new knowledge you are acquiring, you know that this is no longer true.

Using this process of clearing fear, you are the one who is in charge, and you are allowing your subconscious mind to release as much information as it can at this time regarding how you really feel about the fear of death. The information which will be revealed is both critically important, and valuable, in the healing process.

Using Myself as an Example

As before, I will use myself as an example in writing the narrative. I will share with you *how I used to think about God,* and how fearful I was to die. Following that, since I no longer fear death, and have transformed those fears into faith, I will share how that was accomplished.

Please be aware that the words I will be sharing *are not how I think about God today.* Rather, the words used below are those that I believed when I first started to clear this fear.

There is a *framework* or mechanism I recommend to use in clearing your fear. I have found this framework to be extremely beneficial even though it may appear to be somewhat burdensome in the beginning. I use it throughout the remainder of the book. I suggest you use it now.

Later, if you choose, as you become more comfortable with the fear clearing process, you can alter or custom design it to your choosing. Your narrative has been designed to fit within this framework.

Framework

The *Framework* to dissect and clear your fear of death and other fearful subjects in the future is illustrated below.

FEAR

1. Briefly identify the fear you are going to write about.

    - I am scared to die because I don't know what will happen to me when I die.

    - Have I been good enough to be saved and go to heaven? Or, will I go to hell? I am scared that I may go to Hell despite trying to be a good person.

- Will I cease to exist?

- When I die, will my inner existence, my consciousness, my personality, will that disappear and be gone forever?

- What will happen to my family and my friends when they die?

- Will I ever, be able to see them again, or will they also just disappear at the time of their death?

REASON FOR SELECTION

2. Once you have identified your fear, and selected the specific key to place it under, then review the questions related to that key in this space.

For example, in reference to the fear of death, as earlier indicated, I selected Key One - Perfect God, after reviewing the questions.

You can then either write the answer to each question, or write a narrative that includes the answers to the questions and whatever comes to your mind. I chose to write a narrative about what I used to believe.

Please remember that the words used to describe my former fear of death per the aforementioned, and the narrative below, is _what I used to believe_ before I worked on releasing this fear. They are not what I believe today.

Today, I no longer have a fear of death because I know all the positive things that await me, although I still enjoy living here on earth, and do not believe it is yet time for my death experience to occur.

Why I Have Been Afraid of God

As I examined the questions, and my beliefs about God, I discovered that I have been extremely fearful about what I have conceived God to be.

I have believed in a God of judgment and vengeance, who is non-loving, and who is more than willing to doom his unwitting subjects to hell when they have sinned.

I guess in many ways I still do.

For example, I have great difficulty envisioning God as being a God of goodness, or anything more than a God of judgment or vindictiveness. I feel separate from God and believe that God doesn't really care about me. I know I am afraid of God and afraid to upset him in any way, shape, or form.

Nevertheless, I know I will have to face God when I die because there will be a Judgement Day.

I am also scared of hell and having to live in such a hideous place in case I fail the test on Judgment Day.

This is the reason I have been, and continue to be, scared of this God. I believe that no matter what I do or say, I could still end up being harshly judged because I know that God is fully aware of all the things I do wrong, even though I try hard not to be a bad person.

He knows, for example, that I don't always treat people the way I know I should.

He knows that sometimes I don't always turn my cheek.

He knows that I frequently swear even though I know I shouldn't.

He knows that sometimes I am jealous of those around me. He knows that sometimes I am willing to manipulate others to get what I want.

He knows that I am afraid to talk with him because I don't want to be criticized or condemned even though I know I should be punished for the mistakes I make.

This is why I am scared of this God. It is also why I am afraid to die.

God is someone I know I cannot manipulate into my way of thinking even though I desperately want to. And, while I am scared of Hell, a part of me is even more afraid, that I may fail to exist after I die.

The thought that I could fail to exist nearly scares me to death. I just cannot conceive of that happening even though I know that God has the power to make it happen.

Even though sometimes I may not like myself a lot, it still scares me to think that who or what I am could be snuffed out and destroyed, and never again exist. Wow! Now, that is really scary.

Unfortunately, as an adult, I have continued to accept these beliefs, even though they were predominately formed when I was younger. These types of fears still bother me a great deal when I allow myself to think about them.

This is why I am scared of death and to die.

THE SPIRITUAL TRUTH

3. Now that you have identified your fear and you have placed it under the applicable key, you need to write about your new knowledge, the Spiritual Truth you are acquiring, in your journal.

   Please be aware that your writing will need to reflect the new knowledge you are gaining about God, the learning system of the universe, and the spiritual truth about yourself, so the words you write can refute the falseness of the fear you have previously carried.

By proceeding in this manner, your fear can be examined in the light of your new spiritual truth. Through this approach, you will be able to heal your former fear. You will no longer need to allow it to fester and create negativity, or additional limitations for you in your world.

The reason this is important is that your subconscious has now, through your spiritual work, released the depth of your fear along with the causes that initially created that fear.

The words you will be inspired to write in your spiritual journal about why the fear you have held is no longer valid, are critically important.

This will be because of two reasons: (1) You will be writing your new knowledge down on a piece of paper, and (2) By doing this, you will be confirming to your conscious and subconscious mind that you are accepting and putting into practice the new truths you are acquiring.

Using myself as the example, now that my old fear of death had been written down in my spiritual journal, it was now time for me to reexamine what I truly believe *my God* to be, today.

We are One with God in all times

It is not possible for us to be separated from God regardless of the number, or type of errors, we make. We were *created* by God's love thought. We are part of God's DNA. That can never change, no matter what we may or may not do or fail to do.

God's substance is absolute Good, Unfathomable Wisdom, and Infinite Energy. This Energy does not, and can never, ever, cease to exist.

Being an essential part of God, it is *impossible* for us to ever, at any time, cease to exist at the time of *death*. When death comes, as it does for all of us, we will simply change form because energy always exists, although it does change form.

When God created each of us as a Love Thought, our Creative Force set us on a journey whereby we could learn to express our perfection in thought and behavior so we could *earn* the gift which had been given to us. This was done at our request of our own Free Will. Our journey has already taken us to many different lives, in many different places, so we could experience different lessons of learning in many different ways.

This time we are living a life experience on earth, based upon the lessons we mastered in previous lives, as well as those lessons we have not yet mastered. This is the purpose of the lifetime we are now experiencing.

In order to experience the lessons of earth, it has been necessary to acquire a human, or earth body. Accordingly, we have wrapped ourselves *inside* a physical human body made from materials commonly found in the minerals of this planet. This is our Adam, our earth man, our clay man. The physical body is similar in many respects to the suit of protection a diver uses to protect themselves against the pressure of the ocean when they dive hundreds of feet below the surface of the water.

Between Lives

Between lives, we sit with our spiritual mentors/guides, those more spiritually advanced than we are and who are further along on their journey to perfection than we are since they have already graduated from earth. We review with them how effective we had been in learning certain lessons from previous lives as well as those lessons we had difficulty in learning.

Based on the review of those life experiences, together, we determine which ones we did really well with. In turn, it is those attributes that will become the future strengths we can bring with us into a future life.

We also review those lessons where we had made errors and need to repeat them so we can transition those weaknesses into future strengths. The repeat areas become the lessons we will need to work on during future incarnations. It is in this manner that we ensure ourselves that we always have more strengths at our disposal than the challenges we choose to confront.

We then collectively decide, based on our prior learnings, which type of human form, sex, parents, and circumstances, would be most effective for us to be born into from a learning experience.

Illustratively, for this particular lifetime, the earth was determined by each of us to be the most effective place of learning so we could experience the lessons we needed to learn. We will continue to experience the lessons that earth can teach us until we graduate from this place of learning and advance to the next higher plane of spiritual existence.

Together, we collectively decide that we will spend the number of earth lives required to learn these lessons - regardless of the time required, because in truth, there is no time or space.

There is *no judgment or sin* in this process, and there is no heaven or hell outcome, except for those who strongly believe in a place called heaven or hell.

For those who do, heaven or hell will be custom designed, by them, through their own thoughts and beliefs; and they will go there until they realize that those places are but an illusion and are no longer needed. The moment they accept this truth, they will be freed from those misbeliefs and fears.

Generally, we live and spend approximately 100 earth years between life experiences. During that time, we are in the *beyond earth* experience. We associate with and study with those whom we had loved while on earth and who had loved us. This includes family members. It also includes our spiritual teachers.

We had known them as our parents, spouses, relatives, and other individuals who were of importance to us during our former earth experience. This family unit generally stays together, although their roles change.

While not consciously aware of it while on earth, the role of the enlarged family unit in our next earth-life experience, as it is in our current life, will be to help present us with the needed love, and/or challenges, to provide the necessary opportunities for our spiritual growth. In turn, we help our other unit members with their own spiritual learning and growth.

Those who are in our family unit this lifetime will continue to be with us after we experience our earth *death* and shed our physical body. They will also continue to be with us, in future life experiences although again they will likely be in differing roles.

The spiritual law, *"like attracts like"* is in effect for everyone, including our loved ones. This means that correspondence attracts: Love attracts love; fear attracts fear; hate attracts hate.

For example, if we are lovingly close with our mother or father this lifetime, and they have already passed on, they will be present to greet us during our *"welcoming party"* when we return to our *spiritual home* following our death. They will also be with us in future lifetime experiences.

Our welcoming party will excitedly be standing on the shore waiting for our ship to come into view to bring us home. They will shout with joy when they see us come into their vision. They will also feel sad when we leave home for our next life.

This will be similar to those who have just experienced our earth death and feel sad at our departure. Then, they will be joyful when they welcome us back as a baby in one of our future lives even though they will not consciously be aware it is us in a different physical form.

The only difference will be that the roles will not always be as mother, or father, daughter, or son. Perhaps our loved one will be the same mother to us, but we will have a different father. Perhaps the individual who had been our father in that earlier lifetime may be our aunt during the new lifetime.

During our earth death, we simply change energy form as we shed our physical body. Sometimes on earth, it may appear that the physical body is in great pain as it prepares for death. However, that is not true. Instead, it is only the physical body's way of shedding itself, so the inner spiritual part of who we are, our soul, can be broken loose and freed of earth's constraints.

It is not necessary that any of us go through that experience, unless for some reason, we have specifically requested that learning. Instead, we can simply know that when it is our time to exit earth, it will be natural and easy. As long as that is our belief and thought pattern, our earth death will be natural and easy.

We work on and study needed lessons with our spiritual teachers in the place where we go after we physically die. We continue this process until we feel we have sufficiently learned our lessons from a *spiritual perspective* and are ready to try them out again, or experience them in a physical setting which is always more difficult.

At that time, we return to earth to once again *live* an earth experience, to determine if in fact we have learned how to master, or perfect, our learnings while in a physical form.

The physical form is necessary because we have to live in earth. It is comparable to an astronaut wearing a specialized suit before they go into space. In essence, the physical body operates as an insulator between our thoughts and our manifestations while on earth.

Your Thoughts Manifest into Form and Substance

The spiritual law taught by Jesus, "it is done unto you as you believe", is always in effect. *Beyond earth*, the moment we think a thought, it instantly manifests, because we are not physical, and therefore, there is no time separation for the manifestation.

It is different because of the density of energy on earth, even though the spiritual law is the same. Our thoughts will still manifest as we believe. The difference is that on earth, *because earth is material and dense*, it generally takes longer for the energy to transform into substance and create the manifestation.

Thank goodness! Can you imagine if every thought that you presently think were to be instantly manifested the moment you thought it!

For most of us, that would mean a whole lot of messes that we would create - and have to fix!

If you have difficulty understanding this, take a moment and look at the thoughts you have had, just *today*.

Have all of your thoughts been spiritually uplifting, positively constructive, and beneficial to you as well as to all of those around you? Or, have you been upset and had any negative thoughts about yourself, or others, today?

If the answer to any of these questions is yes, remember, those thoughts would have already manifested in your world if you were today living *beyond earth.*

You probably also would have experienced a *whip-lash* in your neck, from being jerked back and forth, so frequently, as your thoughts bounced back and forth!

Thank goodness this does not happen while we are here on earth. Instead, it is to our benefit that while on earth, even though the same spiritual law is always in effect, it is your *dominant thought pattern*, not your individual random thoughts, that manifest in your world. And, while they will manifest, it generally takes longer on earth than beyond earth for the reasons we have shared.

When we are once again re-born into the new earth body we selected while we were beyond earth with our spiritual teachers, we come with one specific objective: To experience those lessons we requested during our learning sessions.

We can never Cease to Exist

During this process of birth, death, and rebirth, *we will never cease to exist* because energy can never be destroyed, or cease to exist. It can only change form, which it and we do, time and time again.

The closest analogy I can make to our being never-ending energy, despite the acquisition of our physical bodies, is to have you recall our earlier discussion of the aliens in the 1985 movie *Cocoon* which starred Brian Dennehy and Don Ameche.

During the movie, the aliens portrayed themselves to be human, with human bodies, and no one was able to tell the difference. Later, it was revealed that the physical bodies used by the aliens were only a wrapping, a suit, around each of them. They were *inside* those human bodies, hidden from view. The life spark, or divine essence, within their physical body wrapping was their unlimited, ever-present, ever alive, element of life. That movie and the vision of life revealed within it is amazingly accurate in depicting who and what we are while we are living on earth.

When we die, the physical wrapping we wore while in that particular life experience, simply decomposes, and returns to the materials of earth.

What *never* ceases to exist is the life force or soul which had been within that physical body.

That life force, that energy, is our *personality*, the *uniqueness of* what and who we are, *our persona, our existence*, which is constantly in the process of growing and learning how to express its perfection in thought, action, and deed.

Our uniqueness, our soul, can never be destroyed or cease to exist. As energy, it simply changes form, dependent on the life lesson being experienced, and the place where the lessons are being learned.

Eventually, that life force which is you and me – will graduate from these experiences and will return to the God head, having earned the ability through our varied experiences, of being able to express the perfection we are in our every thought and action.

We have Nothing to Fear about Death

Therefore, we have nothing to fear about the death experience. In reality, death is no scarier than when we transitioned *from beyond earth* into a baby; when we transitioned from the baby into an infant; from an infant into a child; from a child into a teenager; from a teenager into an adult; from an adult into middle-aged; from middle-aged into aged.

Now, it is but a matter of when it is the appropriate time, to transition into death; which will simply be a transition into a new form of life.

We can never cease to exist, because God can never cease to exist.

God will not judge us because God is incapable of judgment since God is only Love and Goodness.

There is also no reason for fear of Heaven or Hell, because they do not exist except in our own minds.

Therefore, we can release the fears we have previously held regarding death and accept the freedom that comes from knowing we are perfect, spiritual, and divine, created by our God Source, and we can never be separated from God.

THE FINAL ACTION TO
RELEASE THIS FEAR

After examining this fear that I have chosen to heal, and using the key to realize the falsity of the claim it has held over me, it is now time to fully release that fear from your consciousness. We do this through a healing prayer using the following seven steps:

1. Step one is to recognize who and what our God is to us

2. Step two is to state what we believe our relationship is to this God

3. Step three is to acknowledge that we have diligently worked on this fear and are ready to acknowledge the falsity of the fear we have been carrying

4. Step four is to acknowledge that we are ready to release it - forever

5. Step five is to state that we are releasing it to the nothingness from which it came, we acknowledge that this has been done, and we are now free to re-claim the space it formerly occupied

6. Step six is to proclaim that this has now been done, and we fill this new void with Divine Love; and we walk forth free, hand in hand with our God, in our newly acquired Spiritual Freedom

7. Step seven is to stand in gratitude and thank our God that this is done and finished

An example of a prayer that I use to practice this act of releasing the fear we have been working on follows:

Beloved Mother Father God (I like to use this beginning because I am recognizing the emotional and intellectual aspects of God as I think into this God substance). You can use any other name for God that you choose. It is your option.

Father, you are Divine Love, Wisdom, Vitality, and Eternal Life. You are non-judgmental, you love me, and you wish only Good for me. You exist in all places at all times. You are the spirit and the essence of the universe. You can never cease to exist because you are all that there is.

I am your son (or daughter). I am your creation. I am the same exact substance you are, with the only exception being that I exist in miniature form. Therefore, I am Divine Love, Wisdom, Vitality, and Eternal Life. I am one with your spirit and your essence. I am your energy, and therefore am always alive. I cannot ever cease to exist.

I have examined my former fear beliefs that you would judge me for my sins following my death and would punish me, including sending me to hell, or snuffing me out of existence forever. After study and prayerful thought, and with your Divine Inspiration, I have come to see and accept the falsity of these former beliefs which were created and accepted by my fear consciousness.

The truth is you love me. You wish only to have me express my goodness. You continuously hold the vision of my perfection as

your vision. Your desire is for me to express all of the perfection in which you created me. I accept that I am well on my journey. I live, and my uniqueness of life, the special spark of God that I am, will always exist regardless of the place I may be living at any given moment of time.

I now, consciously, release these fears and clear their tentacles from my being – forever. I acknowledge that releasing these fears has created a void within my consciousness that was previously occupied by these fears.

I know that nature abhors a vacuum, so I now consciously reclaim this space and fill it with the constructive energy of your Divine Love. Love is an energy form that allows me to manifest those things of Good that I now choose to manifest in my world.

Father, as I speak these things, I know that they must return to me fulfilled. This is your Divine Law and I know and accept this to be the truth. Therefore, I stand in gratitude that this is done. I walk forth in the freedom of knowing these former fears are no longer a part of my world and have been vanquished to the nothingness from which they came.

Thank you, Father, that this is so. I speak these words and know according to your Universal Law that they must return to me fulfilled.

And, I stand, believing, and accepting that it is done as it has been spoken!

As you finish this prayer, sit quietly and let the Infinite speak to you.

This prayer may seem formal to some, so please feel free to adapt it to your own words and style. I personally like organization and structure so I am comfortable with it.

However, if you are not, change the words to what becomes comfortable for you. The importance is that you use it.

Objective and summary of this chapter

Through using the process practiced in this chapter, you can begin to identify and heal each and every fear that you have brought with you to earth this lifetime.

I have written a longer narrative than what you will likely use. The reason is I took the opportunity to share additional teachings and information about death, its purpose, how it occurs, what takes place after death, and the Creative Source that is the all-knowing energy of our universe. I have done the same in the following two chapters using keys number two and three.

I assure you that using this step-by-step process will allow you to identify and heal each fear you have chosen to bring to earth with you, or that you have chosen to enlarge and expand since you have been on earth.

Enjoy your journey to clearing your fears and re-claiming your freedom!

USING KEY NUMBER TWO

"Who sees all beings in his own self, and his
own self in all beings, loses all fear."

—Isa Upanishad

We are now ready to use the second key and demonstrate how it can be used to heal another of our common fears, one that is applicable to this key. This time, our example is the *Fear of Authority*.

Framework

FEAR

1. As before, briefly identify the fear you have selected to heal and are going to write about

I am fearful of others around me who appear to be bigger, or more powerful than me. I have had this fear for years.

This includes my boss. He has the power to make me happy or miserable. He can even fire me anytime he decides he doesn't like something I do.

I feel the same in many ways about my parents. Sometimes they are great, but other times they want to boss me around. They get upset when I don't behave the way they want me to.

They even tend to pout about it afterward if I don't take their advice. I think that is their way of punishing me. However, it does make me feel guilty, even though I am now an adult. So, I try to behave as they like me to.

I have similar feelings about my part-time college instructor. I feel like he controls my grades and if I don't do what he wants me to do he can flunk me. If that happened it would mean that I would fail to earn my degree.

I guess I am scared about a lot of people, especially those who are in authority positions. This includes the fear of being audited by the IRS, potentially being sued by someone, or having someone falsely accuse me of something over which I believe I have no control.

2. Now that the fear has been identified that needs to be healed, and now that (in this illustration) the decision has been made to place it under key two following a study of the various questions associated with each of the three keys; the next step is to write your answers to key two questions on paper in your spiritual journal

266

Again, this can be done on a question/answer basis, or in a narrative form. As in the prior chapter, I have chosen to use the narrative form and integrate my answers to the questions within that format.

I will continue to use myself as an example since I feel I am an expert in this subject due to the number of years I had suffered from this fear. The fear of authorities was one of the fears I had chosen to bring to earth with me this lifetime so I could heal it. It also had been accumulating from prior lives. That was why it was so deeply rooted in my subconscious this time.

Again, as in the previous key, please keep in mind that the words shared here are the words that I u*sed to believe* - not what I believe today. I healed this fear after working on it for a period of time because it kept cropping up in different shapes and forms so I could eventually heal it at the tap root level instead of at the blossom or stem level.

Fears can Try to be Elusive and Escape Your Grasp

Fears can take on disguises as they attempt to camouflage themselves from you so you can't always get a solid handle on them. Because they are elusive, you may think that you have healed a fear only to have it crop up later in a slightly different form. For example, you can heal the fear of your parents as an authority figure and believe you have healed the fear of authorities.

The truth is - you did! You healed yourself of the fear of authority that was your parents by using this process.

However, the challenge is that you may not have healed your fear of authorities who are your boss, the IRS, or your professor. That is why we have stated repeatedly that the tentacles of fear grow and expand.

The Perfection of the Universal Learning System

When you healed your fear of your parents, you healed the fear which was at the top of the plant, at the blossom level.

Once you heal the original fear, you gain strength in your fear-clearing process. Accordingly, you have the strength to again face the same fear of authorities, but at a deeper level. For example, the next time it may manifest in the form of an overbearing uncle who uses money as leverage over you, your boss, or an IRS audit. Continuing this example, your next fear clearing healing will take place at the stem level of the plant.

You build up your strength from healing each progressive fear on the overall subject of fear of authorities. When you do, you add muscle strength to the previously atrophied muscle. It atrophied because you weren't using it to clear your fears.

The more strength you accumulate, the more you will have the ability to fully combat the fear of authorities until you defeat it at the taproot level. Then it will be vanquished from your world forever.

That is what I did, but it took time. Again, this is an excellent example of how the universe works in its perfection with the learning system and how it becomes customized for each of our individual use.

Because the fear of authorities was one of my deep-seated fears, one which had taken lifetimes to accumulate, it took me a longer time than normal to clear the accumulative fears that had been built up.

The universe was fully aware that while I could heal this fear in its entirety, it would take me some time to build up my muscles, while concurrently building the confidence to do so.

In other words, the strength I was accumulating to conquer future fears in this area grew every time I healed a fear in this subject, no matter how small or large it was. Simultaneously, the confidence in my fear-clearing abilities also grew from these experiences.

I will also share with you that over time, as a new form of fear with a different authority figure popped up in my world, I eventually learned to make it a fun game. Once I had gotten over the original deep-seated fear I held, and had gained confidence in my own fear-clearing ability, I could begin to laugh at myself when the new experience popped up.

Then, with the new genuine confidence that I was gaining, I could say, based on my prior experience, "Thank you Father for bringing this new experience into my world. This is a good thing. I am excited this new episode has come so I can see how much I am growing so I can use my new strength to also heal my fear of this kind of authority."

And, I knew, based on the new strengths I had accumulated, that I could. So, I did!"

Therefore, each time that the challenge reappeared in a different form, I was able to say, "This is a wonderful thing that is happening because I can now defeat this fear, at this new and deeper level!

Please be aware that when it is a deep-seated fear with numerous tentacles that have probably been created over several lifetimes, it may take longer to heal since it can readily appear in many different forms until it is healed at the taproot level. For example, you can heal the fear of one authority figure and feel you have healed your fear of authority figures in general; only to have another fear of another authority figure pop up so you can resolve your fear in that situation as well.

Eventually, using this process, you will completely eradicate all of your prior fear of authority figures. However, it may take different experiences to do so. Or, at least, that is what happened to me.

I am sharing the words as candidly as I am in anticipation that they will be helpful to you as you go through your own fear-clearing process.

I believe these words will also serve as an excellent example of the place a fearful mind can go if it has not yet healed a given fear.

That is the reason we never want to allow any fears to linger in our consciousness any longer than necessary.

REASONS FOR SELECTING KEY TWO

3. Why have you accepted this key? Please write your narrative.

I realize I developed a fear that those whom I believe have authority over me may decide that they don't like me, and in turn, may decide not to treat me well. In essence, I guess I feel in many ways that I would be powerless against them if they were to decide that for some reason, they really don't like me.

I know that I have the ability to attempt to manipulate them, and could try, but I also know that even if I did it would not necessarily work in my favor.

I also fear that anyone in authority is probably smarter, or a better decision-maker, or knows more than I do. Accordingly, I have to do what they tell me to do or I could make a bad decision; or they could decide to hurt me in one form or another.

These are the reasons why I selected key two as the solution to this fear.

As I continued to analyze and think deeper about the questions associated with key two, I also came to the realization that I had created a base of fear around me in terms of how I view others in general. This is especially true with *anyone* that seems to have any kind of authority over me whether it is my boss, my professors, or my parents.

I guess in many ways I am really afraid of them because I feel they could somehow injure me, and I feel powerless to stop them if they decided they wanted to do that. Perhaps that is why I try so hard to please others.

It probably is also why I am always somewhat surprised when my boss or someone in authority compliments me for something I have done; because a part of me really doesn't really expect that to happen, and that is why I have to keep working so hard to always please others and stay on their good side.

I have also learned that I want to be liked, and I fear that if I don't do what others want me to do, they may not like me. This makes me feel inadequate in many ways, or at least not in charge of me, when I am around them. A part of me believes I need to "behave" in the manner in which they want me to behave, so they will just accept me and not want to hurt me.

I also am afraid that sometimes I don't always know *how people want me to behave*. When I feel that way, I realize I could accidentally make a mistake and invertedly make them angry.

The trouble is that because they are inconsistent in what they say or do, it is often confusing. It leaves me feeling afraid to make a decision, because if I do, I don't know how that will affect them or how they will react at that moment. So, I tend to avoid making decisions for as long as I can.

I now see how this fear of others, especially the fear of authority figures in my world, is also negatively affecting my self-confidence and decision-making. For example, sometimes, instead of doing what I believe is the right thing to do, I end up doing the opposite if I believe it will please the person who is in authority.

So, I guess, in terms of the question about whether or not I believe my fellow man, all of mankind is good, I would have to say, no, even though I do believe that most people really do try to be good to others as long as it doesn't hurt them by being that way.

Having carried this fear with me for many years, I realize now that I have allowed myself to accept the belief that other people are smarter than me, can make better decisions, are in control of what I do and say; and I have believed myself to be helpless to try to change it.

THE SPIRITUAL TRUTH

4. Now that your fear has been identified, and you have determined the reasons why you have placed it under this key, you need to write a narrative about the real Spiritual Truth that reflects the falsity of this fear, so it can no longer continue to fester and create negativity in your subconscious

My narrative is as follows:

Now that I have written my fear of authorities on paper, it is now time for me to reexamine what I truly believe, today, about other people, especially mankind in general.

The spiritual truth is that *all mankind has been created by a God of absolute Good.*

Mankind has been created Perfect, but not yet by Expression

God created man as a love thought. Therefore, *all of God's creations* have been conceived in absolute perfection. No one can lose this perfection, this unlimitedness, because it is a permanent gift from our Heavenly Father.

However, this does not mean that mankind has yet evolved to the point that they are fully, or consistently, able to express this gift of perfection. In other words, all of mankind has been created perfect by Creation, by design; although not yet by expression or behavior.

When God created mankind, our Creative Force set all of us forth on a spiritual journey whereby we could *learn, in this learning universe,* to express our perfection in thought, and in behavior; so we could *earn the gift* we had been given at conception. Our journey has already taken us to many different lives, and to many different places, so we could experience different lessons and forms of learning. This is true of me, and you, as well as all of mankind.

Challenges are Designed to help us Change and Grow

In order to demonstrate the spiritual strengths, we have acquired, it is necessary that we have opportunities that provide us with the stimulus for growth. I call these episodes *challenges* instead of problems, because *problems* are difficult to solve and require more energy for their resolution.

Challenges are much easier. If there were not any challenges, man would have a strong tendency to procrastinate. In other words, mankind, in general, has an innate ability to try to put off making a decision, or taking an action, until he is *forced* to do something about a given situation.

This refers back to what we talked about earlier regarding the Change Formula: Unless we have sufficient Dissatisfaction with the way things are, we are likely not willing, or interested, in considering making a change.

This is the precise reason why *challenges* have been designed or created to be a part of the divine learning experience, the spiritual journey we are on. *Challenges are a good thing* in that they stimulate us into making change and taking action. When our challenge reaches the point that it is very uncomfortable, or it becomes unbearable, that is the point when we will act and begin to address the fear(s) that are associated with the challenge.

It is important to recognize that *challenges are not caused by God.* Earth has a tendency to blame God for challenges, especially when they are big. When they are big everyone calls them *problems*, or catastrophes, like when a tornado, hurricane, or earthquake strikes. Earth even calls them "Acts of God".

Always remember, that challenges, or problems, are *not* caused by God. *They can only be created by man.*

In other words, challenges are always created, and can only occur, by the people who populate our world. They may be our bosses, our children, our parents, or someone else.

Large challenges that we experience in our world are discussed and designed *before the earth experience occurs.*

In other words, it is determined while we are *beyond earth* that we need to come to earth in order to grow spiritually in certain areas. We determine those growth areas in conjunction with our spiritual mentors, our teachers, our guides, while we are *beyond earth.*

The One who brings You the Challenge has tremendous Love for You

Also remember that the only way particular growth opportunities, or challenges, can be presented to us, or can manifest in our earthy world, is through another human being. While we personally are the ones who agree to have the challenge presented while we are in the spiritual classroom *beyond earth*, the challenger also has to at that time agree that they will be willing to present the challenge to us during this earth life.

That is not necessarily an easy thing for them to do because they really have to love us to do it. The fact is the harder the challenge, the more the challenger really has to love us to bring that challenge to our doorstep.

The truth, spiritually, is that the more difficult the challenge the challenger presents to us, *the more they love us,* because the more difficult the challenge, the more opportunity we have to grow spiritually. In other words, our challenger would never have been willing to *upset* us with the particular challenge they bring to our attention if they did not have tremendous love for us, despite their not remembering it while they are within the consciousness of the earth plane.

In essence, they have so much love for us that they are willing to play their role masterfully in manifesting the challenge even though they take the risk that on earth we may not continue to love or even like them afterward.

Nevertheless, they are willing to do it because their love for us *on a spiritual level is so great*, even though in their earth body and mentality, they are not even aware their challenge is a *gift, let alone their spiritual role in bringing the challenge to our attention*.

Given this knowledge, I can tell you I MUST REALLY HAVE HAD SOME CHALLENGERS, who have truly loved me, a whole bunch! Because they have certainly brought me some mighty big challenges over the years!

The knowledge of the challenges we are talking about and the role of others in this process is important, because when another person brings us a challenge, we need to first take a moment and remember that the challenger is just like we are - *a perfect child of a Divine Source*- who created both of us in perfection.

The challenger is also like us in that they are in the process of learning to walk and express their perfection, just like we are doing, while undoubtedly making errors - just like we are doing.

This knowledge in itself gives us a much different perspective of mankind, and the role that man plays in our life.

Previously I would have thought that someone in a position of authority was trying to hurt me because they brought me a problem (or challenge) that I resented, and was afraid to face. Now, with the expanded knowledge that I possess, I understand that *I was the one who asked* for the challenge because I wanted to use it as a growth experience.

Further, the fact that they were willing to bring me the challenge, even if consciously they were not aware of it, meant that they really loved me deeply, otherwise, they would not have actually carried out their assignment.

That is a totally different interpretation than I would have had without this new knowledge.

Previously, instead of blessing both the messenger, and the challenge, I would have likely reacted from fear; and detested both the messenger and their message.

The probability is also high that I would have continued to operate from the premise that all mankind would likely, periodically, continue to bring me bad, scary, news. That would have simply increased the preponderance of bad, scary things coming into my world – because through my belief and thoughts – I was the one who was asking that they manifest themselves in my world!

In turn, I would have transferred my fear not only to that individual challenger, but also to all people whom I interpreted to have authority over me. Now, I know how totally incorrect that would have been.

This is the reason why the first thing I always try to do when a challenge is brought into my world is to instantly *thank God for the challenge, no matter what it may be*, and then to name the challenge, as well as the challenger, *Good*.

The reason I immediately name it good is that I know that whatever I choose to name something in my world, it will manifest that name and those attributes. For example, if I name something good, it must manifest and bring forth good. In contrast, if I name something bad, it must manifest that negativity in my world.

Allow me to clarify. Today, with the knowledge I have acquired, I know that God is Good, and only Good. Therefore, I acknowledge that God is in everything that takes place in my world – *even challenges*. By claiming nothing but good in the challenge, I also acknowledge that *God is with me* and *will always be with me,* despite the concern associated with that challenge.

As I name the challenge good, it essentially means that I am stating that *I walk with God, within the protection of God nothing can happen to me that is less than good; and that I will have the confidence and be inspired to know how to handle the challenge.*

God Answers Prayers through People

Another very important thing to be aware of in reference to mankind is that God only answers prayer through people. So, when you pray, you will only see your prayer manifest through others.

This is another aspect of the divine learning system that I love, and get excited about, because it is so perfect.

Remember, if prayers are only answered through another person, then that person must also be in contact with the mind of God, or they would not be able to respond to you in response to your prayers.

Therefore, once again, the fact is reinforced by Divine Mind, that mankind, in general, is part of God; which means that all of mankind must be good and reflect the goodness of God, even if they may not have yet learned to consistently express it.

The sooner we can come to the understanding that all of mankind is an integral component of God's Creation, the sooner we can lose our tendency to fear them, judge them, or speak ill about them.

The spiritual truth is that we are all a part of *Shared Humanity*. The more we can understand this, and put this knowledge into practice, the higher our spiritual consciousness will soar.

One of the best ways to understand and appreciate our shared humanity and the goodness that mankind is, would be to gather together a group of like-minded people for a class in spiritual discussion, meditation, or prayer. Gathering people for the purpose of sharing their divinity is a powerful way to create a shared community with one heart. Illustratively, if you and the group were to read a chapter from this book and discuss it together, or a portion of a chapter at every gathering, you would discover how real key two becomes as the group shares their spiritually uplifting vibration with one another, while concurrently everyone shares *their* humanity and *their* goodness, with one another.

Returning to the role of the challenger for a moment, it is important that we acknowledge that the challenger is also a part of God. God created the challenger at the same time the Creative Force created us. Therefore, we know that God created all of mankind the same as Itself with Divine Goodness and Unlimited Love.

Based on this knowledge, let's use an example of the challenger who fired me while filing a lawsuit against me, which resulted in several counter lawsuits also being filed. Let me assure you that he *must have really had a great love for me beyond earth*, because I certainly had trouble immediately finding the good in him, as well as the good in the challenge he brought into my world, despite my immediately naming it good.

I will candidly share with you that I had to really, really seriously work on myself in order to see the good in him and in the situation. I also had to diligently work the keys in order to dissipate the fear that began to build up inside of me.

While in the consciousness of the earth, it appeared that my challenger had great power over me because he had become an owner, and my boss, when I sold the company. I had a legal obligation to work for his new organization for one year. Instead, I ended up working for him for two years at his request, since he had told me it would personally be of great assistance to him and the company if I did. I had even agreed to work part-time as a consultant to the company when I left.

In addition to being my boss, it appeared that he also possessed additional power over me since he was the one who determined my salary, benefits, bonuses, and later, filed the lawsuit against me.

However, the spiritual truth is that no one has power over any of us *unless we voluntarily choose to give it to them.* God created each of us Perfect. God created each of us with the same Divine Intelligence, Power, and Spiritual Goodness. Our Creative Force did not create one smarter than another, one healthier than another, one more prosperous than another. Each of us was created perfect and unlimited, the same perfection which is in each of God's creations.

It just sometimes appears that way while we are in the conscious of the earth, since some use more or less of the intelligence, health, or prosperity they have at their disposal, than others.

We each have the same ability to accept the ideas and images that we learn and hold in our minds of good, and then transition those thoughts into the realm of imagination and thought – so they can materialize in our reality. The only question is whether we choose to use those same abilities to create the good, the abundance, the loving relationships, the health, the self-confidence we want in our world; or do we choose to give our power away to others so we are unable to manifest these positive attributes due to our fear.

The Person Living under a Bridge

The only real difference between people is where they are in terms of their spiritual growth and how adept they have become in learning how to express their perfection.

Illustratively, a person who is dirty and who is living under a bridge holding up a sign that they are hungry and need a job may be highly spiritually evolved; and have already conquered an innumerable number of fears; even though they don't consciously or spiritually know it given their current earth circumstances.

In essence, they may have conquered every spiritual challenge earth has presented them, except for the remaining lesson they are experiencing and need to solve before they graduate from this earth's plane of existence.

In other words, they may have chosen a life experience while they were beyond earth, where they would be living under a bridge to be learning *compassion*; and once they do, they will be free of the earth plane and its limitations.

But you and I don't know that about them – which is the reason we cannot ever *judge* anyone else, or even judge ourselves for that matter because we don't know our entirety!

Since none of us are able to see the *full spiritual dimension* of another person, we can never know the lessons, the fears that they have experienced, or that they have already conquered. This is why we cannot *walk in their moccasins, or judge them, because we don't truly know them and never will in terms of their spiritual growth.*

Accordingly, we don't have the ability to judge them.

It is for the same reason, that we are unable to effectively judge ourselves, since we are not consciously aware of all of our life-times, nor all of the lessons/challenges/fears we have experienced or conquered.

This is the reason why any form of judgment, regardless of whether that judgment is pointed at mankind, or at ourselves, is wrong. It is necessarily incomplete and inaccurate; is *not a positive spiritual thing to engage in* since we don't know the challenges/ or fears others have accepted to work on during this lifetime, nor the ones they have already healed during their former lives.

Every Person is a Part of Our Perfect Divine Essence

Since every person is a creation of our Perfect Divine Essence, all mankind must be a part of the goodness of God. Everyone is in the process of growing spiritually and learning more and more how to effectively express the spiritual perfection that they are. Some are spiritual infants, while others are spiritual adults.

Once I was able to finally accept the truth of these words I had just expressed, I came to believe that my challenger was not a bad person and really did not want to harm me.

Instead, he had been a blessing to me, and he continued to be a blessing, just in a different manner than I had previously envisioned. He was simply acting out of his fear, as I had also been doing. The spiritual truth was that both of us, through our fears, had caused the lawsuit to manifest, even though he was the one who officially filed it.

As I changed my belief, about both of us, I was able to release my fears. He may also have been doing the same. As a result, we were together, able to settle the lawsuit and the counter-lawsuits out of court. If I had not spiritually worked on both of us, I doubt this would have been the outcome. I believe it was our spiritual selves, our higher selves, that decided to resolve the challenges which allowed each of us to move on with our lives.

While I personally would have preferred to leave the business in a different manner, it ultimately ended up being a real blessing for me. Like everything that happens, we are the ones who may choose which lens to view a situation through; and then through that lens determine whether to name it good or bad.

Being terminated allowed me to immediately sever my ties and obligations to the business, and under court order, not communicate with company employees or customers of the business.

It also eliminated my obligation to work in the role of a part-time consultant which I had previously agreed to do for the new company. As a consultant, I would have felt the obligation to continue doing my very best which would have limited my ability to seek my next right place and career.

Being removed from the business in this manner gave me the instant freedom to completely transform myself into a new career where I now build large, environmentally green, residential new homes; a career that I thoroughly enjoy, without the stress and tension of managing a large number of employees, dealing with Congress or its affiliates, or with executives from prestigious companies throughout the world.

Today, I hold no animosity toward this individual.

Instead, I truly bless him, because he has truly blessed me.

When we settled the lawsuit, we shook hands and we both, sincerely, wished one another the best going forward. I also know we were both simply acting out our fears, until we decided to heal those fears, and express our spirituality. I truly wish him, and his company, nothing but the very best in future endeavors.

Our Challengers are usually those in Authority We have been Fearful of

In the midst of a challenge, it is important that we remember our challenger(s) in a positive light since they spiritually volunteered to give us the challenge. We need to bless them for two reasons:

1. Because we *are the recipients of their gift*, which is a blessing to us, and

2. Second, the positive energy we manifest in blessing them will assist us to resolve the challenge much quicker than it would have been possible to have accomplished otherwise.

I am also the first to admit that sometimes this is not an easy thing to do.

Nevertheless, every one of our challengers deserves our spiritual appreciation and love – while here on earth - if possible.

The spiritual fact is that the harder the challenge, the more the challenger loves us, *beyond earth*. And, if we cannot fully appreciate their gift while we are on the earth plane, we will; when both of us are again together *beyond earth;* and can more readily see with the Eyes of God while understanding the reason behind the challenge.

We next need to recognize that God created you with the same personal power that he has for others.

You can continue to give your power away to authority figures until you come to the decision that you don't want to do that any longer; and that you no longer feel a need to continue that practice.

When you come to that time of understanding, you can reclaim all of the unlimited power that you had previously given away!

The most important thing to recognize is that authority figures, your boss, your parents, or your teachers, are not bad or evil people. First, they could not be *evil* people, because evil does not exist except in our fearful minds.

God is Perfect and only Divine Goodness, therefore evil cannot exist.

Second, the authority figure you fear can *sense* when you are scared of them because you subconsciously give off a *vibration of fear* they can pick up on, regardless of their psychic ability. Your vibration is that strong!

Once *they know you are scared of them*, they know you *have chosen* to give away your power to them. And, I assure you, the vast majority will be very happy to take it from you since few ever refuse this gift.

Always remember, *you are the one* who chose to give up your power to them so they can determine how *they* want to use your power – *not you*. They are not bad people. They are the same as you since they are also on their spiritual journey. They are not better nor any worse.

Spiritual Practice with an Authority Figure

Whenever you are dealing with an authority figure you fear, I suggest you step back from the situation regardless of whether they are a boss, teacher, or parent.

Get away from them physically for a moment, go to a quiet space, and sit in silence. As you do, envision them in your mind's eye as being a spiritual creation of God, the same as you. Draw their *essence and being* to you in prayer.

Speak to them in your prayer and tell them you are sorry you gave them your personal power out of fear. Inform them that you have now decided to reclaim your power, which you are now in the process of doing, based on your new learnings.

The most effective thing you can do as you release your fear of them in your prayer, is to recognize you no longer have a reason to fear them.

Instead, since you and they are both spiritual beings, created by the same God, begin the process of seeing them in their spiritual perfection. See them in their strength and their beauty - but also see your own beauty and strength.

See them loving you as you love them. Send them this vibration of love and surround them with it.

They are not stronger or more important than you, nor are they any lesser.

Recognize that they are also children of God on their Divine Pathway, the same as you. Wish them only the best for their life and progress, and ask them in prayer to help you learn how to become a better employee or a better student, and how you can be of better service to them and the company if they are your boss.

As you surround them with love in your meditation, see them encircled with this vibration of goodness that you are sending them.

Then, thank them for the experience and the challenge they have provided you, and know that perfect right action will take place.

Continue to steadfastly hold this thought and belief about them regardless of what happens in the physical. *Know it to be the truth.* Continue to hold them in love within your thoughts.

Obviously, you do not want to discuss any of this with them verbally, because the challenge is being resolved in the spiritual realm so it can manifest in the physical.

Now, step back in the physical and watch and observe. Changes will begin to take place for the better as you consistently hold these thoughts, although initially it *may* appear to get a little worse.

The reason for the temporary worsening is because you are changing the vibration you are sending them and they may not immediately be aware of how to react to it.

However, as they do adjust, you will see the situation improving little by little until the situation is resolved. If not, rest assured, God will move you or your current boss to the perfect right position.

Do the same with any authority figure you fear. As you do, watch and observe what takes place. I have watched this phenomenon take place many, many times in many different settings. The boss may change. The employee may change. Both may change. The employee may be offered another job in the same company, or with another company.

Bosses can change dramatically

I have seen bosses who initially appeared to be "jerks" to their employees, transition into becoming their mentors. I have also watched employees move on to other far more pleasant working environments.

Again, like attracts like. When we send out vibrations of fear, we must attract back fear. When we send out vibrations of love and goodness to everyone, even those we previously feared, we must attract back this goodness. It is the spiritual law of the universe.

I personally have had a lot of experiences working for whom I initially thought were bad bosses. *I guess, beyond earth*, I must have requested that I have this experience many times so I could thoroughly learn the lesson, which meant I had a deep fear of authority figures I needed to clear.

I had a boss who detested me before he even met me

As an example, I even once had a boss *who detested me before he had even met me. How about that for fun and jollies!*

289

That happened because the individual who had hired me into the business world from academia had left the company by the time I reported to my new position.

My new boss informed me upon the first day of my arrival that HE would never have hired me, HE thought I was a terrible fit, and that HE planned to get me *fired* as quickly as he could.

To make matters worse, I soon learned that his reputation was that no one should ever cross him or do anything in any way that would tick him off because he had the ability to get anyone fired that he wanted to and he had the power and standing in the company to accomplish that result.

How is that for a nice way to be greeted on your first day of work when you are already nervous about transitioning into the business world from academia. Right?

However, using these spiritual principles, I came to the conclusion that my new boss was giving me a special gift of informing me that I had to do an exceptional job in my new position, even though I had never previously worked in the business world. I knew that despite his animosity, I could spiritually earn his respect, or that the situation would have to change in one form or another; even though he made a conscious effort of completely avoiding me while offering absolutely no constructive comments or suggestions whatsoever.

As a result, I did a whole bunch of praying for him, and me, and for the situation I found myself in. I also want you to know that if my prayers would have made him holy, he would have been the holiest man to have ever lived on earth!

Every time I began to fear, I surrounded my new boss and the situation with divine goodness and inspiration and knew that God was in charge.

As a result, I was *inspired* to individually go to the managers that I was going to be teaching in my management development sessions before the classes started, sat down with them, and asked them to share the problems they were experiencing in their work units so we could collectively solve those problems in the class. They readily gave their permission to do so, and we did. It turned out that the problems they were experiencing were similar in many respects to those also being experienced by other members of the class. As a result, the material I was teaching became extremely relevant and was no longer simply "academic theory".

As a result, the managers who had their problems solved were pleased, and they became very vocal about this "new guy" who personally spent the time to understand their managerial problems, and who had helped them solve their issues.

Other managers in the class also became highly vocal with their praise in that they had observed special problem-solving techniques that worked in real-time, and they commented that they were, or had, already started to apply those techniques in their own work units. The word spread, and my boss kept hearing the praise I was receiving.

Concurrently, I kept being approached and asked to develop solutions to new problem areas as challenges arose in the business. In this manner, I quickly gained a reputation as an individual who was not afraid to solve real-time problems facing the business.

The president of the company learned about my success with his management team and asked me to represent the company in Washington, D.C. together with other executives from the general aviation industry and assist them to develop a strategy that would resolve long-term problems they were experiencing. I was able to use my academic skills and former training to assist in determining solutions for the business in which I was employed as well as in Washington while I continued to learn and develop new business skills.

As a result, the boss who detested me, could not stand my sight, and wanted to get me fired, transitioned into becoming an incredibly strong fan and personal mentor; got me special bonuses and raises; and turned out to be instrumental in getting me promoted to corporate.

In contrast to originally being scared of him, I truly learned to love him. I sincerely missed him when I was promoted to the corporate offices 1000 miles away. We tried to stay in contact despite him continually giving me a hard time now that I was technically "one of his bosses". We stayed close until he left earth.

To this day I feel very affectionate toward him, send him prayers, and thank him for his blessings; because in retrospect, they were truly a blessing.

The Spiritual Laws

The spiritual principles we are discussing - work - because these are God Principals, and God Principles, the Spiritual Laws, always work. We just have to take the time to apply them and then hold in faith until they manifest in earth through the density of the vibration of earth.

These are the same spiritual techniques that I used with my former boss who had sued me. They are the same spiritual techniques you have the opportunity to use with any authority figure(s) in your world that you have learned to fear or give your power to.

Authority figures, as well as all other people, always correspond with love energy, whether it is your parents, your relative or business colleague who you believe has wronged you, or your boss. Remember that each of these people was created Perfect by God, but like you, they have not yet learned how to consistently express their perfection in their thoughts, actions, and deeds. While they are still on their pathway to perfection, they will receive the divine love you send to them, even if they choose not to use it this lifetime.

Also remember, that you are the one, not them, that chose to give your power to them, the power God gave you when your Creative source brought you into existence. You are the one who made this error - not them.

You are *also the one that now has the ability to remedy this any time you choose to do so.* The power you gave away did not leave *permanently.* It only *"temporarily" left,* since you asked the universe to temporarily give it away for you.

You - have the strength of God behind you to gain your power back - whenever you choose you want it back!

Previously, you gave others your power because you were fearful, now, you no longer choose to be fearful. Therefore, you can reclaim your power, and the power over your life, any time you choose to do so. It is as simple, or profound, as that!

You have also created a fear of not being genuinely liked or loved by others. Watch and observe as you pray and release your fears, how in turn, you will attract those who love you - by the new vibration you are creating which surrounds and permeates you and your being.

As you chip away your rough edges, your flawed marble edges, and release the magnificent David inside, others will automatically be attracted to you and to your magnetic vibration of goodness. Remember, fear attracts fear, while love always attracts love.

THE FINAL ACTION TO RELEASE THIS FEAR

5. After examining the fear I had allowed myself to accept about authority figures, I have now chosen to heal myself of this fear.

I am using this key to realize the falsity of the claim that fear has held over me. So, it is now time to fully release that fear from my consciousness. *We do this through a prayerful meditation something like the following* (please use the words you are personally comfortable using.

Beloved Mother Father God

Father, you are Divine Love, Wisdom, Eternal Life, Goodness, and Power. You have created me and all of life through your Love Thought. You love and wish only Good for all life and all mankind whom you have created.

You also love and wish only Good for me as part of your overall creation. You have created each of us to be unique. All of us are uniquely precious to you. You exist in all of us at all times. You are the spirit and the essence of all Mankind. You are the life I feel inside when I place my hands over my solar plexus. We exist, because you exist.

I accept that all of Mankind has been created Perfect. Man is in the process of exploring this gift and each is on a spiritual journal to perfect their Divinity in their thoughts and deeds. I accept that Man has not yet achieved this state of perfection, and will undoubtedly make errors on an individual basis during their exploration, the same as I do. We are all in the process of recognizing and manifesting our perfection to the best of our abilities.

I am your daughter (or son). I am your creation. I am the same exact substance you are with the only exception being that I exist in miniature form. Therefore, I am Divine Love, Wisdom, Vitality, and Eternal Life. I am one with your spirit and your essence. I am one with your energy, your power, and therefore am one with your life force. I cannot ever cease to exist, nor can mankind cease to exist, because we are all part of the same substance of God. We are all One with you.

I have examined my former fearful, false beliefs, that others, especially authority figures, including my parents, my bosses, and my teachers, are more powerful than me; and I have to be nice to them and obey them for them to like and accept me without hurting me.

After prayerful thought, and with your Divine Inspiration, I have come to see and accept the falsity of these former beliefs which were created by and through my own fear consciousness. The truth is you have created all of Mankind, and all of Mankind is in the process of learning to express their perfection in their thoughts and their actions. Spiritually, we all love one another.

Others wish only Good for me. I wish only Good for them. God has placed other members of Mankind in my world to help me grow spiritually. Others are assisting me to learn and grow on my spiritual pathway and are reaching out their hands to help me on my journey. I give thanks to them for so loving me that they are willing to do so.

No man is stronger than me because I walk with the strength of God. However, I can give my power and strength away, and I now see how and why, through my own fears, I have chosen to do so.

I have now grown spiritually, and I now consciously choose to reclaim my strength my power, my self-confidence, and the belief in my own abilities and decision-making. I know your desire is for me to express my perfection, my power, and my strength in my every thought and action until I fully express all of the perfection in which you created me. I accept that I am on my spiritual journey, as are my fellow men. I acknowledge that I live, and my uniqueness of life, the special spark of God that I am, exists in all Mankind, and will always exist within each of us regardless of the place we may be temporarily living in at any given moment of time.

I am now ready to release these fears and rid myself of them. I now, consciously, release these fears and clear their tentacles from my being – forever. I acknowledge that releasing these fears has created a void or vacant space within my consciousness which has been previously occupied by these fears.

I know that nature abhors a vacuum, so I now consciously reclaim this space and fill it with the constructive energy of your Divine Love. Love allows me to manifest the things of Good that I now choose to manifest in my world.

Father, as I speak these things, I know that they must return to me fulfilled. This is your Divine Law and I know and accept this to be the truth. Therefore, I stand in gratitude that this is done. I walk forth in the freedom of knowing these former fears are no longer a part of my world and have been vanquished to the nothingness from which they came.

Thank you, Father, that this is so. And it is done, as it has been spoken!

USING KEY NUMBER THREE

"Fear defeats more people than any other one thing in the world."

—Ralph Waldo Emerson

We will use another example, in this chapter, of a common fear which is health. Since my personal health has not been a major challenge throughout the majority of this lifetime, I have used an example from one of my earlier patients. I am using her words in this chapter but, for obvious reasons, without using her name.

Framework

FEAR

1. Clearly identify the fear you have selected to work on and briefly describe that fear in writing in your spiritual journal. My patient said:

I am fearful for my health. I have diabetes. I have gout. I have high blood pressure. I am obese.

Since God has given me so many health problems, I guess I must not be a good person.

Now, I am afraid I have cancer. I am scared to see my doctor because if he tells me I have cancer, I know it will be a death sentence. I know that chemotherapy will make me sick. I will lose my hair, I will look awful, and then I will die. I'm scared to die. But I also know I can't continue not seeing my doctor.

I have had these kinds of health problems all of my life. I am at my wit's end about them and I don't know what to do anymore. My church tells me I am supposed to just accept these health problems and the pain caused by them as part of the cross I have to bear in silence. So, I guess I am even violating that by talking with you.

It is as if my health problems dictate everything about me and are in charge of my life. Now, I might even have cancer on top of everything else!

SELECTING THE CORRECT KEY TO PLACE YOUR FEAR UNDER

2. Now that the fear has been identified that is in need of healing, and now that (in this example) the decision has been made to place that fear under key three, perfect man, after a discussion of the various questions associated

with the keys; the next step is to write down in your spiritual journal answers to key three questions.

Again, this can be done on a question/answer basis, or in a narrative form. As in the prior chapter, I have chosen to use a narrative form to describe and integrate my patient's discussion about the questions.

As my patient answered the questions, we both began to realize how separated she felt from God. She had created a base of fear around her health, and in a way, felt that God had given her health problems as a *"cross" which she was supposed to bear as a penitence to God. She had learned this from her church days. She had also been taught that she had to bear her penitence to Jesus, or the Cross, in silence, without complaint.*

The church has taught her that the reason she continually experienced various health problems was that she was a sinner and still had a lot of sins that had to be forgiven. Bearing her health problems in silence was her way of being forgiven by Jesus so she could be saved. That was *supposedly* the reason she was to bear her cross in silence.

As she expressed these feelings, she readily admitted that she even felt *guilty* talking to me about them because, perhaps, her discussing them out loud was a violation since she was not continuing to remain silent about her suffering.

As I listened (the more you listen to another person the more you will discover that they will give you the solution in the words they speak), I learned she was scared to death she would get cancer because her grandmother and mother had had breast cancer and they had each died from it. As a result, she had come to believe that if she got cancer, it would be fatal because her belief was that everybody who gets cancer dies.

She felt powerless to stop the disease if her doctor diagnosed her with cancer. In other words, it would be like a death sentence.

In summary, she told me that she felt vulnerable, especially with all of the health issues she had, felt she was not a good person, and she believed that God and Jesus had forgotten her, or at a minimum, expected her to *bear her cross of ill health in silence.* She even reluctantly admitted that sometimes when her husband got drunk, he would physically beat her. The fact that he verbally put her down was just something else she had been taught that she had to accept and bear as penitence.

As we continued to talk, she also admitted she was afraid to die because she believed that God would continue to punish her with even more illnesses because she had not continued *to suffer her health problems and other problems in silence as she had been told to do.*

She felt worthless and her self-confidence and self-esteem were about as low as they could be. Summarily, she did not feel good about herself in any area of her life; certainly, did not believe in a God of Good; or that God could love her, and could never be separated from her; because she knew she was a sinner, and a bad overall person, even though she said she tried to be a good person much of the time.

THE SPIRITUAL TRUTH

3. Identify the spiritual truth underlying the fear that has been chosen and write a narrative about it in your spiritual journal.

In this instance, we chose to use the third key since the primary fear my patient was experiencing was her personal health – especially with the possibility of cancer. However, the more she talked and answered the questions associated with this key, the more her fears grew into her fear of her husband and other people which is key two, and about God, which is the first key. As a result, it was necessary to use all three keys to be of assistance to her.

By the way, this is not terribly unusual. Frequently, one fear may escalate into other fears which means that more than one key will be involved. When that happens, the determination under which key to place the fear should be made based on which key is primary. For example, in the illustration with my patient, her primary fear was her health and cancer which was key three.

Because of the numerous challenges that my patient was exhibiting, it was necessary that we explore each in-depth in order to help her heal. For that reason, the narrative we have written as the spiritual truth is very expansive and encompassing. I have left it in this form because it is believed the information is inspired and pertinent to our learning.

In general, there are three areas that have been designed to help you to grow spiritually as an individual perfect creation of the Divine Source while you are here on earth. You will discover that every single challenge you will ever experience will emanate from one or more of those areas; which will always be for learning growth opportunities. The three are: (1) challenges with physical, mental, and/or emotional health, (2) challenges with relationships, and (3) challenges in the form of prosperity, with prosperity being far more than economics.

Some choose to use all three of these challenge points for growth. Some only choose to use challenges with health, or relationships, or prosperity. For example, you may have chosen not to use health as a challenging point this lifetime for your learning and instead have chosen to concentrate on abundance and relationships. Or, in contrast, you may have chosen to only concentrate on one of the three areas in order to stimulate your spiritual growth.

My patient had chosen to grow spiritually, predominately, through health challenges, her fear of God, and her husband. So, my role, as her therapist, minister and healer, was to help her become aware of the fears she had created concerning her health, God, and husband; and to discover where those fears had originated. In turn, we could begin the process of writing her narrative regarding the spiritual truth. By so doing, we could help her eliminate her fears and help her prevent continuing to fill her consciousness with negativity; which was the causation factor behind her continued health issues and abuse.

As I helped her dig deeper into her fears, I helped her realize that her fears were grounded in her belief that the health problems she was experiencing were much stronger than she believed herself to be. She felt powerless against them. She believed that God was punishing her. She believed that her health challenges were punishments from God that she had to accept, since she was not a good person. As a result, her self-confidence was very low.

Fears associated with health are primarily based on two beliefs: (1) Believing we are separate from God, and (2) Believing that health challenges are stronger than we are to heal them.

Also remember: Fear is false earth information that appears to be real.

To begin our work, we first needed to reexamine the relationship beliefs she had about God. The reason we needed to do that was that like many of my patients at that time, we had to come to an understanding that in contrast to many beliefs we still hold about a vengeful God, God *has not, and does not cause any negative* health *issues or negative problems of any kind against us. We do it all by and to ourselves.*

God *does not* punish us with health. Therefore, God does not need us to punish ourselves with any form of *penance* in order to be healed, or saved.

The fact is we are, and have *already been saved* - because God created us in perfection, and our Divine Nature *is* Perfection. We do not need to do a single thing, certainly do not have to "carry a cross" to achieve this state of consciousness, because we are already *perfect by design and by origin.* All we have to do is to learn to fully express it in our daily thoughts and actions.

The spiritual truth is that our God, yours and mine, is Absolute Good. God has created each of us as a love thought. There is no way that we can be separate from God -_except in our own beliefs.* Regardless of whether we believe in God or not, God *always*s, *at all times, believes in us.*

And, God always exists in each one of us.

That is the reason that when we go into a church building, God *is in that church*. The reason God is in that church *is that we carry God* into that church with us. When we go to a museum or sporting arena, God is in that building because we carry God into that building with us.

My patient, along with the vast majority of patients I have ever worked with, has a strong tendency to use words that continue to attract the challenge to them that they want to heal. In other words, through the words they use, they keep telling the universe, and then continually reinforcing it, that the disease they have, or the poverty they have, or the abusive relationship they have - IS THEIRS –they OWN it – and they want to continue to OWN it!

Let me explain by explaining how this is done and why the *I AM* is so incredibly powerful. Those two words are the most powerful words in the universe. They are the *hidden name of God*.

When you use those two words, you are claiming and affirming your Divinity, your Godliness. The words you use immediately after the I AM, affirm to the universe *what it is you want, so it can manifest it for you*. For example, when using the I AM for health, speak forth words like "I AM healthy; I AM expressing forth my outstanding health in all ways; I AM strong; I AM my perfect weight; I AM filled with God's energy.

When using the I AM for self-confidence and self-esteem, speak forth words like, I AM serenity in my world; I AM blessed; I AM wise; I AM talented; I AM inspired; I AM disciplined; I AM able to make appropriate and wise decisions; I AM self-confident.

When using the I AM in relationships, speak forth words like, I AM beauty; I AM attracting nothing but love to me in all ways; I Am drawing loving relationships to me right here and right now.

In areas of abundance, use the I AM and speak forth words such as, I AM abundance, I AM wealthy, I AM as abundant as the leaves on a tree, I AM seeing cash money freely flowing to me from all directions which gives me the freedom I desire.

These are all positive words and statements, and they will create love and good for you in your world when you allow them to manifest as you clear more and more of your fear.

But, because of the power of these two words, you also need to be very careful what follows your I AM. In other words, *you do not* want to follow it with such words as I AM not healthy, I AM sick, I feel crummy regarding my health, I Am suffering with pain, I have gout, I AM experiencing migraines; or with such negative statements as I AM broke, I AM ugly, I AM unlucky, or, I AM in debt. Unless, of course, you want those things and desire to have them manifest in your world.

If you have been using negative affirmation words, with your new awareness, you can now change those words to positive. Start to become very sensitive and aware of the words that you use. When you do, you will begin to change the existing conditions in your world, including your health. This is what I counseled my patient in reference to the words she had been using. She consciously began to make the necessary effort to change her words going forward, as she understood how *she was causing* the health challenge, not Jesus, and not God, which kept her in physical pain and abuse.

Each of us has been created in absolute Divine Health. The reality is that you cannot lose this state of health, because it is a *permanent gift* – one which we have been given from God – unless like some have done with their personal power - you choose to give it away. And, based on Free Will, that is always your option, as you can attract to yourself whatever it is that you request through your belief.

You can also decide with your spiritual mentors, while *beyond earth*, that you desire to have certain health challenges when you re-enter earth as a baby so you can grow spiritually from overcoming those particular challenges. When that occurs, they become part of the learning process you created before coming to earth.

Those health challenges will manifest, *not as a punishment*, but as part of the learning process you chose to create during the life you are living. You do not need to continue to accept them, as you have requested that they manifest so you can learn to heal them.

This is true regardless of whether it be physical, mental, and/or emotional health. Again, it does not mean that you have to accept the health condition, whatever it may be. You have asked that it manifest so you can learn from it, and/or heal it, that is its only purpose. As you learn the lesson, you have the option to heal the condition.

Please also be aware that some may choose to keep their current health challenge because they believe they can better accomplish the lessons they came to earth to learn with their current health issue than without. That was the reason Jesus always asked those he was about to heal if they wanted to accept the healing before he sent them healing energies.

There is nothing wrong with keeping the existing health challenge as long as the patient realizes that any condition can be healed if they desire it to be healed. Also remember, God has *never* created any health condition that you experience. *You* are the only one that has done this. Accordingly, you are the only one that has the personal ability to heal the condition or to ask a healer (whether it be a medical professional or spiritual healer) to help you accomplish this result.

In essence, your Creative Source has blessed *you* with *perfect health along with the Perfection of Being.* It is *God's desire* for you to express this heath in all good ways. The All-Knowing One envisions for you that you are able to walk in total freedom with, and at, your perfect energy, weight, and nutrition.

God wishes you to have excellent health which means to be *in harmony* with your living environment. God does not wish pain for you in any way, shape, or form. Nor, does God expect you to express any form of penitence in order to be healthy, or prosperous, or to have loving relationships.

For example, I have never met anyone whose pain makes them more God-like. Pain only exists as a signal that you need to change something you are doing. It is like a traffic light. You only need to remember that when the traffic light is red, it will soon change to green. The truth is we are one with God. God is our strength and power at all times. We just need to learn to express this belief in love, in abundance, and in health.

Living with a human body gives us spiritual opportunities to experience what it means to be healthy while living on earth. Health challenges provide fantastic learning lessons and are one of the major reasons why we have chosen to wear a physical body during the experience of living this lifetime. But they only need to be *temporary*.

Health challenges provide short-term, but *immediate feedback regarding how we are doing on our spiritual journey.* Furnished with this information, we then have the opportunity to change course as needed.

If you have health challenges, or a lack of prosperity, or are lacking in loving relationships, it simply means you have created those conditions through your thoughts so you could learn and grow. When you become uncomfortable or dissatisfied with any, or all of those conditions, it simply means that you need to identify your fears in those areas and clear them.

Then, with and through non-fearful, loving thoughts, and unfiltered positive energy, you can change those conditions for the better and remove the challenge. This is how strong and powerful your God has created you to be, with your creative strength and power.

When you request, claim, and affirm what you desire, and hold in faith; it is a spiritual reality that your prayers will be answered as long as you believe they will be fulfilled.

Your spoken words are like prayers because your words are spiritual, and they will manifest through the energy that is Perfect God energy (key 1), which is continually manifesting throughout the universe. The *conditions within your personal world* have been predicated by your thoughts (key 3), because your thoughts are based on God Energy – and - they are that powerful!

When your thoughts, your prayers, are answered, as they must be, *they will always be answered by and through other people* (key 2). The reason this takes place is that as your fellow man, shared humanity, answers your prayers, it provides you with the opportunity to experience and learn that every person in your world is part of a perfect God (key 2) and therefore, is perfect, spiritual and divine – just as you are (key 3). This is an example of how the three keys are stand-alone, but also perfectly align with one another when appropriate.

For example, our physical bodies have been superbly designed to bring us immediate and astonishingly valuable feedback. If our health is in excellent shape, we know we do not need to make a change because we are being productive on our spiritual pathway in this area of learning. In contrast, if our body manifests an ailment, it tells us we have some kind of issue we need to heal. Nothing more. Nothing less.

Similar to the electric stop light on the street, health issues provide us with a signal we need to heed. If the light is green, it means everything is going fine and we should continue forward on our spiritual journey. If it is a yellow light, it simply means we can proceed forward, but need to be cautious and aware something we are doing may be a cause for concern in the future. If the light turns red, it means we should immediately stop and examine what we are doing, because something is not working and it is taking us off of our growth pathway. As one of my dear friends once told me, our bodies have been *"perfectly designed to create the results they produce"*.

Without these mechanisms, we could be *operating blind* in terms of how effective we are in manifesting our individualized perfection while we live here on earth. Without the speed dial on our dashboard, we might have to wait until after our physical death, *beyond earth*, before we could effectively evaluate the spiritual progress we are making, or failing to make here while on earth. Instead, thanks to this form of feedback, along with other forms including inspiration, dreams, meditation, and prayer, we may keep our foot on the gas pedal, or take it off, dependent on where we are in our spiritual progress or deviation.

Personal challenges are controlled by our thoughts and beliefs, and they become indicators. Our physical bodies have specific *spiritual health equivalents for learning purposes*. These spiritual equivalents operate in a similar manner to the stop light in that they give us green, yellow, or red signals in the form of minimum, moderate, or severe health challenges in the physical body.

For example, if you have fears regarding *your future*, your body will manifest a physical ailment with your *feet or legs*, because those parts of your body are represented by the spiritual equivalent of "fear *of the future*". Illustratively, you may manifest a swollen foot; a sprained ankle; gout; or a broken ankle. Any or all of those symptoms are designed to inform you that you have created a fearful thought about the future; one which is in need of being cleared and changed. Remember: None of these are punishments, they are only indicators,

In other words, if your misdirection is only slight in terms of your fear of the future, you may manifest a bruise on your leg. If it is a moderate misdirection, you may experience a swollen foot or a mild case of gout. If it is a severe departure from the path, you may find yourself with a symptom such as a broken ankle, foot, leg, or a severe incredibly painful case of gout.

We create our own health challenges. God does not do this to us!

Since we are the ones who create the health challenge with our thoughts and beliefs, we are also the ones who can clear the fear underlying the spiritual equivalent and heal the condition *before* the fear has had an opportunity to cement itself in our conscious and subconscious minds.

As we clear the fear underlying the spiritual equivalent of health, the health ailment can be healed. It is only a question of how much time we believe the healing will require to manifest. For example, I have been involved with healings that were instant, some that took a while to manifest, and others that took a long time to manifest. The length of time involved had to do with the belief held by the patient, not with the earth-defined severity of the health challenge.

Another example of the physical body providing a lesson for spiritual growth is the *arms and hands*. This part of the physical body has the spiritual equivalent linked with *a fear of giving and receiving*. Illustratively, if we have a challenge in our ability to *give to others*, it means we have created an erroneous fear belief that God *does not* have sufficient love, or prosperity to go around, and therefore, we have to "*tenaciously hold on to everything we currently have, or otherwise we will find ourselves going without.*". This is a condition often associated with selfishness and tight-fistedness. This condition is not only associated with money. It can also mean that you are not willing to give of yourself in terms of your inspiration, your wisdom, your love, or your time.

The *fear of giving* is experienced on the right side. If the fear is not severe, it may manifest in the form of a rash on the right arm, a bruise, a sprained wrist, or a hand. Conversely, if your fear of giving is more pronounced, it may occur in the form of a severely swollen or broken hand, wrist, or arm.

Fear of receiving is the spiritual equivalent linked to the left side of your body. If you have challenges *receiving and accepting praise or gifts from others*, the expression will be in your left arm or hands. For example, if you have a minimum amount of fear, the health symptom may manifest in the form of a bruise, sprained wrist or hand. In contrast, if you have significantly veered off your spiritual path, it may manifest in the form of a broken left wrist or arm.

Diabetes is another spiritual equivalent. Diabetes can manifest when we have "*lost the sweetness in our life*". In other words, if we manifest fearful thoughts of believing that living has become dire and depressing, and is no longer exciting or uplifting; we may manifest diabetes to let us know we have gotten off our spiritual path. If it is only a minor departure, it may appear in pre-diabetes which is easily healed and remedied. If a more severe departure, one featuring a form of depression or suicidal thoughts, the condition may manifest in a more severe form requiring insulin shots.

Another example is H*igh blood pressure.* The spiritual equivalent is "*suppressed anger, or hidden fears of anger toward another.*

The person we are expressing anger toward could also be ourselves because we might believe we may have failed to do something correctly, or we may be angry because we are procrastinating to avoid doing something. Or, it may be that we are angry with someone else. Or it could be we are angry at many people. *Suppressed anger is always fear under pressure,* where physically, we tightly squeeze our blood vessels due to anger.

Obesity is a common ailment in today's world. The spiritual equivalent underlying obesity is *a fear that we are vulnerable to others, are defenseless, and are not protected.* Obesity becomes a justification to overeat and add layers of fat around our physical body in an artificial form of attempting to protect ourselves against others. It is an attempt to try to create an insulation of protection between us and those we are fearful will hurt us.

Those who experience this health condition are reacting out of fear of the world they are living in and are trying to protect themselves from others or from God.

Remember: God is our source of protection, not our layers of fat. God created us, always sees only the best for us, and is always present to protect us as long as we choose to accept it to be so.

I stop here for a moment and will share that I worked specifically with the patient in reference to the spiritual equivalents for diabetes, high blood pressure, obesity, and gout, since she was experiencing health challenges for each. As we helped her understand her fear and the spiritual equivalents, we were able to help her heal each of these conditions as she realized that her health challenges had not been caused by God, but by her own fearful thoughts and beliefs. Therefore, she could heal herself of each of these conditions. And, she did. We also used the healing prayer which is at the end of this chapter.

Alzheimer's is a disease that is becoming more and more common in society. The spiritual equivalent of Alzheimer's is someone *who has lost their quest for life, an individual who no longer has a dream to live.* It is not difficult to understand that many who have to live in a nursing home, frequently without visitors, manifest this illness.

When I was a dean at an academic institution, I used to request, when possible, that our professors, when teaching a subject such as American History, invite the elderly who had lived through the Depression or World War Two to join their classes and share their personal experiences of what it was like to live during those times. Invariably, some of the students in the class, intrigued by the older person, or out of kindness, would invite them to the cafeteria for a cup of coffee or coke afterward.

This resulted in the older person inviting the student(s) to their home for milk and cookies, which frequently created an ongoing relationship. Such experiences resulted in their having young visitors to their home, which in turn helped them shed their loneliness and feelings of no longer being needed.

Later, I learned from several of their relatives that some of those elderly "teachers" had begun to exhibit early stages of Alzheimer's prior to being invited to participate in the classroom experience. Those conditions disappeared as the elderly person knew they had something to contribute, knew that they had to stay alert to teach in the class again, and knew they would continue to have frequent visitors.

Physical ailments, such as these examples, are designed to be "*temporary*". They can be healed no matter what the ailment may be if we consciously choose to clear the fear and accept the healing. Or, they can become "*permanent*" if we believe they are necessary. It is our decision, and our decision alone, to decide how long we choose to allow a certain physical ailment to persist in our world.

God did not create the ailment – you did!

However, God can help you to heal it – if and when you desire to have the healing take place.

There is no right or wrong in God, nor is there any time in God. Time and space do not exist in the spiritual dimension. We choose our fears and we choose our time frames, the amount of time it takes to heal our fears. It is up to us. In terms of healing, God finds no difference between a hangnail or cancer.

Both are simply physical ailments that we have created as teaching lessons. Both are physical conditions that can be healed as soon as the lesson associated with the spiritual equivalent is learned. All we have to do is to learn the lesson, clear the fear associated with the spiritual equivalent, and allow the condition to be healed. It is as simple - or as profound as that.

For example, if we have a sprained right wrist, the moment we choose to work on the fear underlying the false belief that "*there is not enough to go around*", and clear it, there will no longer be a need for the physical ailment to continue and it can be healed. As soon as we learn the spiritual lesson, release the fear, and fill the new vacuum in our consciousness with love, we can be freed from the ailment since the spiritual lesson will have been learned.

The physical body has been designed by our Creative Source to continually be in a natural state of divine health. Thus, the physical, emotional, and mental bodies are designed to be responsive to healing.

God works through medical doctors and nurses as well as other forms of healing. For example, when I am sending healing energies to a patient who is going to have an operation, I pray that the doctor and nurses performing the surgery will be blessed with God's healing energy, that they will know what to do through God's divine guidance, and that their hands will become the healing hands of God.

As I have worked as a minister, therapist, and healer, I have found that the amount of time required for physical healing to manifest is based upon three factors: (1) the current thought pattern of the patient (2) how firmly the patient is holding on to the fear underlying the spiritual equivalent(s) and (3) how willing they are to release their fears and accept the healing.

It is also important to remember, to avoid any form of judgment. For example, in some cases, a patient may choose to hold on to an ailment and choose not to heal it this lifetime for various reasons. Illustratively, they may choose to *work on it this lifetime* and then continue their work with it *beyond earth,* so they can heal it in a future life experience. Remember, it is always *their choice,* and it is necessary to avoid any kind of judgment regardless of whether it is with us, or the patient, in terms of their healing process.

It has also been my experience that animals and babies are usually the quickest to heal because they have not yet developed thick layers of fear, or earth's belief in the rejection of healing energies. Therefore, they are generally much quicker to accept the healing energy and manifest it in the form of healing than others.

An example is the healing that occurred with our puppy Tasha, a beautiful silky terrier whom Susan and I dearly loved. Animals are psychic and Tasha was especially so. Animals have not accepted earth's teaching that supposedly no one is psychic and that healings do not exist.

Tasha was psychic, knew I was a healer, and whenever she was not feeling good, she was eager to have me hold her and give her healing energies. She was always eager to receive those energies and was quick to jump on my lap to accept the healing. She always allowed the healing to quickly manifest, no matter what her health challenge may have been, because she knew that condition was just temporary.

This process continued until her last days when she was 14 years old. Susan and I had been at the island and were just returning. We had not taken Tasha with us because the trip would have been too taxing for her. Instead, she stayed with Susan's mother and my brother-in-law, both of whom dearly loved her. As always, she was thrilled to see us when we returned.

However, on this occasion, she was not as energetic as normal with her greeting. I began to give her healing energy but she was not receptive. It was the first time in 14 years that she had not positively accepted the healing energy.

The next evening, she was in great discomfort and we had to take her to the urgent 24-hour veterinarian hospital. Susan drove and I sent Tasha healing energies during the trip, which she again chose not to receive. As I psychically tuned in to her, I began to realize she was in the process of leaving her physical body.

While I didn't want to accept this and kept sending her healing energies, the doctor soon confirmed my suspicion as he informed us that Tasha had an advanced terminal condition and was in pain. Her recommendation was that we should immediately put her to "sleep."

We decided to wait for a few hours and have her see her normal veterinarian before making that decision. He confirmed the diagnosis. I psychically tuned into Tasha again, and she told me it was time for her to leave earth, she was ready to make the transition, and she would return in the future. So, we tearfully had her put to sleep. Susan held her while she left earth.

I now understood why Tasha had chosen not to accept the healings I was sending her. Instead, she had chosen to have those energies go into her spiritual bank account and be stored for her future lives when she could use them as she chose.

We were in grief with her passage, but we both knew she had brought us great love and joy. She had determined it was time for her to leave earth and continue on *her* future spiritual journey. We also knew the spiritual law, *Love attracts Love,* is always present. Tasha loved us and we loved her. As a result, we know she will be among our loved ones jumping up and down in joy to greet us at "our welcoming Home Party" when it is time for each of us to leave earth, our temporary home, and return home.

Another health example is a baby who as a patient had been brought to me with jaundice, a condition where the child's skin turns an unnatural yellow in complexion due to liver or bile duct issues. Because the baby had only entered earth about three months earlier, she had not yet created an earth veil of fear around her and was highly susceptible to healing energies. As a result, by the culmination of our session, the baby had accepted the healing energy, and the session ended in what earth refers to as "*an instantaneous healing*".

Any healing can occur as soon as we accept it. It can also manifest as quickly as we believe.

The same is true with cancer, although to many, cancer *has become much more than a disease*. While it does have the same objective, which is to bring our attention to the fear equivalent that needs healing. However, it is significantly different from other physical ailments for one reason: Race Consciousness, or the collective consciousness of mankind, has created an *especially thick layer of fear* around this disease, far more so than other physical ailments.

Cancer had become the most fearful disease a person could possibly get – at least that was *until Covid-19 struck*! Now, it has been forced to accept second place. Nevertheless, the word cancer still has tremendous fear tightly wrapped around it and it is still accepted by many as being a death sentence, despite the many advances made by modern science to combat it.

The doctor becomes God: the cancer diagnosis becomes a death sentence.

It does not have to be that way. Now that we have new knowledge we are gaining in this publication, we need to recognize the spiritual truth about cancer. Cancer, like any other ailment, has simply come into existence for us to learn from and heal. Like other ailments, it notifies us that we have made a significant departure from our path, and we need to make a change. It is our choice whether or not we choose to do so.

The spiritual equivalent of cancer is *a blow to the ego that has never been healed and which has recently been activated. The equivalent then focuses more specifically on where cancer has struck, and why it has occurred in that area. For example, stomach cancer would be the equivalent of a blow to the ego which has been recently activated that the recipient cannot stomach.*

But just like any other physical ailment, we can release the fear associated with it, learn the lesson, and heal the condition. Healing must occur with cancer just as it does with any other physical health challenge. It is as simple - or as profound, as that.

Learning lessons associated with physical ailments also apply to our emotional and mental bodies. Illustratively, I had a 6-year-old child who was brought to me as a patient because he had a tendency to start fires in his home, or anywhere else, whenever he could find matches or a lighter.

As we worked together in therapy, he was most effective in communicating by drawing on a piece of paper the fears he was experiencing which revealed the underlying reasons why he was starting fires. Through therapy and drawings, he was able to release his fear of feeling unimportant and unwanted. He had been starting fires because he knew it scared his parents and it got their attention. Previously, they did not share outward attention, or affection with him; and he had felt unwanted and unloved. Once he started fires, he got their full attention so he kept doing it.

Over the course of several sessions, either with him, and or with his parents, we were able to examine and alter the conditions which had caused the abnormal behavior on his part. As the underlying fears were resolved, both the child and parents were healed, and his desire to start fires never returned.

Challenges, whether they be physical, mental or emotional health; relationships; or prosperity; are only learnings that manifest through our fear to provide opportunities for spiritual growth. That is their only purpose. It does not matter in terms of health whether it is a hangnail; sprained ankle; gout; diabetes; high blood pressure; anger; cancer; depression; schizophrenia; or Alzheimer's. To God, they are all the same.

Either the patient alone, or with the help of those who have offered to be of assistance to them by channeling the healing energies of God, can heal a broken ankle, cancer, or the virus as quickly as a hangnail, regardless of whether the condition has occurred in your own body, or in another person's. It makes no difference to God. The condition has only occurred as *a temporary lesson* to be learned, and as soon as the lesson is learned, the condition can be healed and the fear resolved forever.

God is present with us at all times. God is Perfect Health. We cannot be separate from God since our God is within, and is one with us, always. Our Creative Source views our health as overflowing in goodness. We can have as much abundance in health, as we can have abundance in prosperity and abundance in loving relationships. We have the ability to pick and choose what we want in our world.

Once our patient was helped to understand where her fears had originated, and that God had no desire for her to continue to punish herself, we were able to look to each health challenge she had exhibited. We examined the spiritual equivalent for each, and we began to work to heal the equivalent, which meant the health condition could heal itself.

After helping her understand and analyze the fears she held, she could begin to understand the falsity that those fears held regarding her health. She also understood that the time had now come for her to release her fears from her consciousness. As she expressed a genuine desire to do so; she began to put her beliefs into action.

Once she reached this state, one where she desired to release her fears, we then held a *structured healing meditation*.

Please be aware that it is important that your patient *hear* your healing prayer as an affirmation of the words you are speaking as you state the word that *your patient is releasing the fears they have held and they are accepting the spiritual truth of their new knowledge so the healing energies can emerge.*

As your patient hears you speak the words of healing, *together with your self-confidence that these words are the spiritual truth,* they will relax and know that you are acting as an instrument of God for their healing.

Again, you can choose your own approach or you can modify the words I used to your own style. I will share the structured healing prayer I used at the end of this chapter. This structured healing prayer is an excellent model to use with your own healing work with others, especially in the beginning, if this is an area where you choose to be of service to others. All of us are healers. Some just like to express this gift more than others.

Our patient, over time, *was totally healed* as she released her fears and replaced them with her new faith and belief in God. Some health ailments she quickly healed while others took more time to manifest. Nevertheless, she healed every health challenge she had previously experienced.

This is how God and healing work. It is *miraculous* in its simplicity because God, despite all the complexity we attempt to assign to Divine Mind, is simplicity in action.

You will also be interested in learning that the patient did attract cancer and she was diagnosed as having cancer by her doctor. However, because she had changed her former fear beliefs about cancer, the form of cancer she had was minor and she was quickly able to heal it; and it never reappeared in any form.

Gradually, she transformed herself from the non-confident, fearful, person she had allowed herself to become; into the magnificent lady who possessed the ability to express the inner beauty she had suppressed and held dormant for many years. As a result, she healed all of her health conditions while concurrently transforming her life. We all possess this same ability.

She also made many changes in her life as she transformed herself from living in fear, into expressing her divine self, through her faith. For example, she had been in an abusive marriage. As she regained her self-confidence, she made the decision that she no longer had to accept that form of abuse or punishment.

As a result of her transformation, her life and her personal world became exactly what she had requested from the universe: Outstanding health; soaring self-confidence, self-esteem, and the belief in her own abilities; a belief that she walked with God as her companion; and a new abundance of loving friends and relationships.

She became an example of how putting her new knowledge into belief and action could manifest into the goodness she had requested. This is how God and healing work. To many on earth it may even appear to be miraculous.

However, it is not miraculous, because *the spiritual laws of God always work, and must manifest, as we believe and clear space in our consciousness through the release of our own fears.*

This is how simple – or how profound - the Learning System of the Universe is.

Believe it, accept it, and your *personal belief and thoughts will, and must, manifest* and transform your individual world!

Following is the structured healing prayer I used:

HEALING PRAYER

Beloved One of All Creation

Father, you are Divine Love, Wisdom, Eternal Life, Goodness, and Health. You have created this one, and all of life, through your Love Thought. You wish only Goodness and abundance of health for all. You love this one as your child (it is suggested that you use their name here). She is an essential part of your overall creation. You have created her to be unique and unparalleled. she is precious to you. You exist in her at all times. You are her spirit and her essence. She exists because you exist. She can never be separate from you because you are never separate from her.

We accept that you have created (her name) perfect, spiritual, and divine. She is in the process of exploring this gift on her spiritual journey. she is also learning to express her divinity in all of her thoughts and deeds. She knows that she has not achieved this state of perfection yet, and will undoubtedly continue to make errors during her exploration. However, she is now fully engaged in the process of recognizing and manifesting her natural perfection to the best of her abilities.

She is your daughter. She is your creation. She is the same exact substance you are with the only exception being that she exists in miniature form. Therefore, we acknowledge that she is Perfect Health, Divine Love, Wisdom, Vitality, and Eternal Life. She is one with your spirit and your essence. She is one with your energy, your power; and she is always aligned with you. She can never cease to exist - because she exists one with you. You and she are One.

She is now examining the former fearful beliefs she has surrounded herself with about her health challenges, her erroneous thinking that her health problems have come from you in the form of punishments that she needed to bear, which have caused her to feel separate from you.

After prayerful thought, and with your Divine Inspiration, she has come to accept the falsity of those former beliefs which were created by and through her own fear consciousness. The truth is you have created her and given her the gift of perfection and set her forth on a spiritual pathway whereby she could earn her perfection.

She is in the midst of this journey of learning to express her perfection. She now knows that physical, mental, and emotional challenges have come to help her to grow spiritually, and she now blesses them for coming into her world as indicators. However, she now knows and accepts that she has created her own health challenges, that they are not created by God, and they are not God's punishments. She has also looked to the equivalents and is now releasing the lessons associated with them so she can heal.

Father, this one (use her name) has now so grown that she no longer needs to hold these health challenges and she can now heal and release them. She chooses to do this at this time. Therefore, we now speak forth the word that these health challenges are vanquished to the nothingness from which they have come – right here and right now!

There are no longer any physical, mental, or emotional challenges, no matter what they may be, or what they may be called, that are stronger than her (use her name) because she now walks with your strength. She knows that she previously gave her strength and power away, but she now sees how and why she had done that, and that it was done through her fear.

She now releases those fears and she grows spiritually. She now consciously chooses to claim her strength and power back, so she can use it for her own healing.

I know your desire is for her to express her perfection, her power, her health, and her strength, in her every thought and action so she can fully express all of the perfection in which you have created her. I accept that she is well on her spiritual journey. I acknowledge that (use her name) lives, and will always maintain that special spark of God that she is, which will always exist with her, regardless of the plane she may be living in at any given moment of time.

She is now ready to release all of these fears and rid herself of them as she consciously clears these enslaving shackles, and their tentacles, from her being and essence – forever.

We also acknowledge that as (use her name) releases her fears she has created a vacant space within her consciousness that had previously been occupied by those fears. She knows that nature abhors a vacuum, so she now consciously reclaims this space and fills it with the constructive energy of your Divine Love. Love allows her to manifest the things of Good she desires to have in her personal world which includes an abundance of positive health, self-confidence, personal contentment, and loving relationships.

Father, as I speak these things, I know that they must return to us fulfilled. This is your Divine Law and I know and accept this to be the truth. Therefore, I stand in gratitude that this is done.

I walk forth in the freedom of knowing that the former fears that (name of patient) had previously carried are no longer a part of her world, and that they have been vanquished into the nothingness from which they came.

Therefore, she is now healed, right here, and right now!

Thank you, Father, that this is so. It is done as it has been spoken, we accept this healing, and we stand in gratitude that this is so!

Amen.

When you finish your prayer, step back, bless your patient, and allow your healing energies to merge with the ones they possess that are being called forth. Remember, their healing will manifest as they allow it according to their belief system.

It is not difficult to become a healer as a therapist or healing practitioner with others, if this is something you genuinely desire to do with the new knowledge you are acquiring.

You can also use this prayer for yourself. I even suggest you record it. Then, while you are relaxing in a meditative state, play the recording so your consciousness can hear and accept your own healing words. This can be done as many times as you wish for your own healing.

As you work with your patient, they will likely begin to see some health improvements quickly, and they may ask you to continue to speak your healing prayer with them, or to continue to share your healing energies. You can also record this healing prayer for them.

I suggest that you always assure your patient that they are in the midst of the healing process, which is in the process of manifesting, because it is, and you are simply affirming this reality for them!

By virtue of your connection with God, you have become God's instrument of healing. As you help others heal, you will also be healing yourself because this is how the spiritual law works.

You are also becoming an Ambassador of God to others.

YOU NOW HAVE THE KNOWLEDGE TO CLEAR ALL YOUR FEARS

"Fear is the main source of superstition, and one of the main sources of cruelty. To conquer fear is the beginning of wisdom."

—Bertrand Russell

During the prior three chapters, we selected three common fears as examples that have been most commonly identified by participants during workshops: The fear of death, the fear of authority figures, and the fear of health.

We then used the framework to analyze each fear and to determine which key the fear should be placed under.

We recommend you initially stick close to the framework as you begin your *personal process* of identifying and clearing your fears. After you become comfortable with the framework, adjust or alter it to your own choosing so it becomes YOUR framework, customized to your own personal taste.

Use of a framework to release your fears is important. However, do not let a specific way of working minimize your interest or diligence. Your interest and willingness to release your fear are what will allow your magnificence to emerge – and that is what is important. Your self-confidence, personal strength, loving relationships, abundance, health, and your well-being are all at stake.

Based on the new, but ancient knowledge, that you are created unlimited, and are just now in the process of realizing and practicing it, allows you to *begin to walk more and more unlimited on earth within your own perfection.*

Again, it is a mathematically proportional relationship – *the more fear you release, the more unlimited you become.* The more fear you release, the clearer you become as a channel to receive. The more fear you release, the more you strengthen your magnet to correspond with and attract the positive things you desire in your world with your thoughts. It is as simple or as profound as this!

Remember, each fear you release - exponentially increases your personal power and your unlimitedness.

Because the earth is the planet of fear, it has created more than 200 individual fears. Regardless of whether the following fears are considered to be healthy or not, they are all fears common to earth, and if you possess any of these – they need to be cleared from your consciousness and healed:

- Fear of being born in sin; dying in sin; fear of being doomed to hell

- Fear of failing to exist when we die; or fear of losing who and what we are, our being, our essence, our personality; at the time of death

- Fear of conflict; fear of losing our job; fear of failure

- Fear of not having money; of losing our home; of being evicted

- Fear of relationships and not being loved for who we are

- Fear of losing self-confidence in our own abilities; our self-worth

- Fear of not being liked or valued for who we are; fear of marriage

- Fear of divorce; fear of attracting a new mate; fear of being alone

- Fear of the IRS

- Fear of health; fear of growing old or feeble; fear of looking ugly

- Fear of speaking in front of an audience

- Fear of heights; fear of insects; fear of lighting; thunder; tornados; hurricanes; or earthquakes

- Fear of flying; fear of the dark; fear of driving

- Fear of riding in an elevator; fear of the water; fear of drowning; fear of confined or crowded spaces

- Fear of food; fear of blood; fear of snakes; fear of needles

- Fear of sleep; fear of germs; fear of strangers

These are only a few of the many fears created by humanity I use as examples to illustrate how pervasive and widespread fears have become on this planet where we are temporarily living.

It is likely that over the years you have chosen to accept some, or many of these as your own, while you have rejected others. The purpose of this list is simply to illustrate some of the many fears humanity has created, all of which limit your ability to express t your fullest capacity.

Each fear you carry, regardless of size or magnitude, limits you from expressing the full unlimitedness in which you have been created by your Divine Source. Since God has given you Free Will, you can choose to fill yourself with fear or love – *but not both*.

You cannot have an abundance of fear, and an abundance of love, at the same time. That is not how you have been designed to function or to operate. Unfortunately, today, the majority of people on earth believe in fear, rather than love. That is why they are carrying out the behavior they are, which is but a reflection of the fear they believe their God to be.

You are a being of light. Your human physical form is just the smallest aspect of who and what you are. Fears such as relationships, abundance, and/or health are only here for one purpose - to be learned from and healed.

There is fear and there is love. There is nothing in between. The more fear you tenaciously cling to, the less love and unlimitedness you will have.

The spiritual truth is that *any limitation you have*, no matter what it may be, goes back to fear.

Remember, fear is false earth evidence that appears to be real.

Earth is unreal, but will nevertheless feed your five senses sufficient faulty information so your *Fears will feel and appear real* – but only from an earth perspective!

The fear taproot runs deep. You have to dig it up by the roots if you want to clear it, or it will keep coming back again and again and again.

More than ever before, the earth now needs you to clear *your fears* so you can *add to the vibration of love* on our planet and welcome earth's transition to the New Age of Compassion.

Just as earth is transitioning and being reborn for the new Age, you also have the opportunity to be reborn and transformed: You can now release the fears that have bound you to the earth plane of consciousness and become the spiritual being you already are, the one who is temporarily walking on earth, in a physical body.

You are living on earth, at this precise time and space, because YOU have asked to be here - NOW. You have *asked* the universe to bring this book to your attention now.

This means *you are the strongest of the strong; and you are now ready* to clear your fears, heal yourself, and express your perfection; while simultaneously healing the planet in its transformation.

Your gaining possession of this book did not happen by accident!

As you take the first step toward achieving *your own unique unlimited state of goodness,* your Divine Linkage will *miraculously* inspire and *bring more and more of your fears to your conscious mind* – so you can clear and heal them.

This will take place like *a magic journey* played out between you and the Divine. You will watch this process take place in a way that will seem removed from everyday life!

You and I are co-creators of our reality – the individualized world you and I have created and live within this lifetime.

There are 7.8 billion people living on earth. No two are exactly the same. God has created every single one totally different, and totally unique. Each *of us is individually precious to our God.* For example, out of the 7.8 billion people, none have the same fingerprints. This is how much God loves you– that he would create each one of us this unique. Doesn't even sound conceivable. But it is!

The spiritual truth is that each is the individual Spirit and the Spark of the Divine that has created us. We are so much greater, so much more than anyone can ever imagine. As we allow the *Divine Magnificence of who and what we truly are* to leave the blanket of fear behind, the cocoon of darkness that we have lived within for so long; we will emerge free and find we now have the wings to soar!

We are each that unique, divine spark of life that has an incredibly exciting journey in front of us as we walk hand-in-hand, in self-confidence, in abundance, in knowledge, in understanding, in love, in health; with our God, who always sees us in our Divine Perfection!

You will soon discover how enormously exciting and magical this journey will become for you.

Heal your fears, align your beliefs with the infinite, refocus your thoughts, and watch your world change for the better as you manifest all that you desire, but had never previously thought possible.

Sit back, enjoy the ride, and watch it *miraculously* take place as you do your part *to emerge from your cocoon of fear.*

Your life will never again be the same!

Earth, and your fellow man, will bless you for taking this journey and sharing your new knowledge, your new faith, your new transformation of self, and your transcendence into self-actualization and personal mastery.

As you do, your energy of transformation will transcend itself and will attract others to the new pathway you have chosen to share with all of existence.

As you learn to fly, you will become God's *Ambassador* to others.

And, it is ended in this time.

ACKNOWLEDGMENTS

I am grateful to many people whose personal interest, assistance, and expertise have been helpful to the development of this book.

First, I want to acknowledge my wife, Susan. She has been invaluable in supporting me as I am again, for the eighth time, reinventing myself, this time as an author. She has been a part of several of these career reinventions while serving as my administrative executive assistant. For example, she performed this role when I was the CEO of an international actuarial software company specializing in retirement when our customers included PBGC, Congress, the White House, Amtrak, Fortune 500 corporations, and major financial centers such as the Cayman Islands and Bermuda. Susan provided her same skills when I transitioned to create our environmentally friendly, green residential home build business. She is now encouraging me in my writing.

My appreciation also goes to Jeff McCrehan. Jeff used to head the FBI speechwriting office and personally worked for Robert Mueller when he was Director of the FBI. He and I are collaborating on the development and professional editing of this and future books. I love bouncing ideas as we interface on how to make this information available. Our mutual interest is to be of service to those looking for their next steps in our turbulent world. This book is an important part of that process.

I am grateful for my sister Kathy Mae. Kathy has faced numerous challenges this lifetime. One of the things I admire about her is that she easily could have become a victim. Instead, she has transformed herself into an extremely talented spiritual teacher who is loved by her students. She serves as an inspiration for me.

I thank Kay Crawford who for years has been a student of these studies. She lives her life to the highest of her abilities as she practices the teachings on a daily basis. Kay has read each book and has offered suggestions and guidance which I appreciate.

My daughter Deborah Gordan, has offered her suggestions, including marketing. She is a talented metaphysical writer and teacher who has always been a special part of my world.

My son Shawn Gordan has been a metaphysician all of his life and is able to reach people I would never be able to reach. He and his friend Charles Robinson have helped contribute to this book by reading, using the exercises, and providing me with their feedback and insight. Their efforts are appreciated.

Special thanks go to our cover designer and graphic artist Tiago Pereira. I am grateful for his skills and talents in helping these books come alive through the front and back covers and professional formatting. I have learned that these skills are critically important in the publishing business. Therefore, I truly appreciate Tiago's skill and his dedication to making these books come *alive* for so many.

I also wish to acknowledge the profound and priceless teachings of my deceased wife Carla Neff Gordan and *the invisible nonphysical spiritual teachers and mentors who worked through her* as an incredibly talented trance medium. I am both grateful and appreciative that I continue to receive that inspiration and guidance.

Hopefully, I have been able to integrate my personal knowledge and experience, together with that wisdom, into these books, so they can be appreciated by those who are ready for this journey of learning.

Finally, I am extremely grateful to be alive, and living here on earth with the spiritual and metaphysical knowledge I am blessed to have received this lifetime. Earth is going through a major transformation, massive change which affects everyone and everything, as it transitions into the New Age of Compassion and Enlightenment. I feel blessed to be a part of this process and am grateful for the opportunity to share my experience with others.

OTHER BOOKS BY THE AUTHOR

THE FEAR-CLEARING TRILOGY BOOKS

△

EXECUTIVE OVERVIEW

My goal in writing the fear clearing trilogy is to send you off on a personal and self-help spiritual growth journey that will transform your life while helping you realize *how special you are*. The books are also designed to help you understand that to be living in this age, at this time on earth, is unique. The service you will provide to yourself through your learning and growth will not only be of great assistance on a personal basis, but it will also go far in helping mankind and our planet heal themselves.

I truly want you to reclaim your personal power, become a more confident decision-maker, healthier, happier, more abundant, and create more loving relationships in your daily living while becoming the person who *"sees everyone around you with the Eyes of God* and *who hears everyone around you, with* the *Ears of God"*.

The more you become this divine expression, the more you will become an Ambassador of God here on earth. You will not only become an example to others, but when it is time, you will also leave this world a better place; because everyone, and everything, throughout the universe, is interconnected. Nothing is separate, or alone unto itself.

We are spiritual beings temporarily inhabiting a human body; instead of a *human who is attempting to become spiritual*.

As you learn to express more and more of your true nature, you will become a Co-Creator – her on earth – with God. This is how much power you possess!

As we acquire new knowledge, and couple it with ancient wisdom from our spiritual teachers and *mentors from beyond earth*, we will *manifest the perfection of who and what we are* here on earth as we accept personal responsibility for our beliefs, our thoughts, and our actions.

I have found in discussions with colleagues and students during classes, lectures, and business settings, that the question is invariably asked, "Why do we, as a species, fail to achieve our vast potential and create wars, poverty, and disease instead; while simultaneously destroying our eco-system"? The follow-on question becomes, "*Do I believe we will ever achieve our unlimited state of perfection?*"

My answer is, *"Yes, we absolutely can, however, we won't be able to do so until we clear the fears that currently enslave and hold us in bondage and limitation"*.

Shared humanity has an *unfathomable ability* to create universal good.

However, when you look at what mankind has achieved during the thousands of years we have walked on earth, our achievements seem pretty puny; especially in comparison to what we could have accomplished by eliminating war, famine, disease; and if we cared for one another as if each were truly our brother and sister which they are since we have been created by the same source.

Our personal growth and the liberation of the entire human race are possible through our collective release of fear.

Working in twelve different countries, whether in business, education, or a ministerial/therapeutic career, I have found that fear, and its taproot, regardless of whether it is called stress, tension, anger, judgment, guilt, or lack of self-confidence; *is the single greatest reason why* mankind is failing to express the vast, unlimited potential that is today fully available to each of us. I believe it is also why I have been spiritually guided to write these books at this specific moment in time.

We are like Aladdin. We hold the magic lamp in our hands. The genie is there waiting for us to request what it is that we want. All we have to do is to believe in the unlimited magnificence that our Creative Force has created us to be to make our request known to the universe and allow it to manifest. When we do, we will discover that there is no time or space in the spiritual world as we fold the past, present, and future into one and become the specialness we each are in truth.

As mankind, we have evolved to the point where the capabilities each of us has available are mind-boggling. We are truly *unlimited*. Unfortunately, that is not what earth teaches nor is it how the vast majority of individuals on earth believe or live their lives, *because we have been programmed and allowed ourselves to be shackled and crippled by fear.*

As the new Age of Compassion and Enlightenment approaches, the time has come to share the wisdom contained in these books.

The trilogy combines the principles of metaphysics, business, psychology, spirituality, and self-growth. Each book is unique in that it provides a look through a different lens, but from the same prism. Each can be read alone, or as a trilogy, because each is an important component in the overall fabric to help *us learn how to clear fear and live the unlimited life of freedom that the absence of fear provides.*

Eight books, in addition to the three in the trilogy, are in the process of being written, inspired by spiritual teachers, and mentors *from beyond earth.* These nonphysical teachers have profound wisdom, and view earth things from an *outside of earth perspective* since they are not limited by living within the fear vibration that surrounds our planet, nor by the Ways of Earth.

An abstract of each of the three books in the fear-clearing trilogy follows:

BOOK #1 OF THE "FEAR-CLEARING" TRILOGY

FEARLESS WISDOM

Transform your Life through Transcendence and a Divine Spiritual Shift

Richard A. Feller, MA, MBA, Ph.D.
Foreword by Alan Cohen

△

The purpose of book one is to provide an understanding of what fear is; how fears have been fostered by earth; and how important it is to release those fears so our spiritual (not religious) self can fully emerge. Specifically, it teaches how to walk on earth as a spiritual being temporarily residing in a physical body by releasing fear and mastering lessons associated with the earth plane.

The book also teaches us about who and what God is. Not the God we have been taught that lives somewhere in the sky and is a vengeful being waiting to judge us. Rather, we will discuss how God is the universal energy that is everywhere, and is in everything. The energy that cannot ever be destroyed, although it can, and does constantly change form. The energy that is all existence.

This book includes the three ancient, previously hidden, secret keys to identifying and releasing fear. The keys have been provided by *spiritual teachers/ mentors from beyond earth*. They had been hidden to prevent persecution by formalized religion since the teachings revealed in the keys are the opposite of what is taught by earth religion and would therefore be considered by many to be blasphemy.

The three keys will allow us to open space in our subconscious mind by releasing our fears, which we can then fill with positive, constructive, love energy. In turn, it teaches us how we can use this energy to manifest the goodness we want in our world, whether it be in the form of abundance, loving relationships, health; or all three.

Book one also shares how we can walk in the spiritual manner in which God intended us to walk, with our divine self, while here in the earth plane.

This book lays the foundation for the second and third books of the trilogy. It is a step-by-step guide in learning how to identify fears we have carried into this lifetime from prior lives, how we can identify them, release them, and then learn how to use that freed-up energy to manifest the things we most desire for our world.

This book has been written, professionally edited and formatted, and will shortly be available through Amazon.

BOOK #2 OF THE "FEAR-CLEARING" TRILOGY

A PERFECT SOUL

Self-actualize yourself and become your own magnificence in the World You Create

Richard A. Feller, MA, MBA, Ph.D.
Foreword by Scott Allan

△

Jesus was serious when he referred to our capabilities as a Co-Creator together with God. He continued his teaching by informing us that *"we could achieve GREATER things than he had accomplished."*

Unfortunately, we have dismissed his words as being illusionary, as much of a fantasy as Aladin and the magic lamp. Instead, we have been indoctrinated by earth to believe and accept the opposite: That we are filled with fear, are limited, and certainly could never become divine in miniature form.

Like ancient alchemists, our spiritual purpose on earth during this life cycle is to turn lead into gold. In other words, we are to transform Adam, the vibrationally heavy clay man of earth; into the magnificent David, the energetically light spiritual perfection whom in truth we already are. Drawing upon transformative principles practiced by the alchemists, this book will help us learn how our core fears have been invented, and then continually nourished; by formalized religion, government, business, and organized crime; so, we will become obedient and loyal to those institutions.

Once we gain a thorough understanding of how and why our governing institutions initially invented fear and the reasons why they continually reinforce it, we will have the opportunity to transform our lives by releasing the core fears they have programmed into our consciousness. As we do, we will fill the vacuum left by the release of that fear energy into the creative energy of the universe, so that divine energy can manifest what we request in the personal world we habituate.

Book two will provide us with the blueprint to achieve *self-mastery or self-actualization*. We will learn how to customize this plan to our individual lives.

The process we will use will include a unique adaptation of the change model the author used for many years to successfully help senior management change and transform business organizations from an economic disaster into success.

It is this model, which has proven to be successful, that we will use to facilitate the successful transformation of ourselves on an individual basis.

This book is finished. It is in the process of being professionally edited. Although the book is not at the moment ready to be published, we anticipate it will be in the near future. Advance orders can be placed through *Richardfeller.com.*

BOOK #3 OF THE "FEAR-CLEARING" TRILOGY

SPIRITUAL MASTERS RELEASED THEIR FEAR

And became Co-Creators with God – So can You

Richard A. Feller, MA, MBA, Ph.D.

△

Greek philosophers taught that every human being is "a microcosm of the macrocosm".

In other words, they believed that *every person is a miniature form of* our Creative Force, whose love thought gave birth to each of us. All it takes to realize the uniqueness each of us represents is to realize that no two humans, out of the entire 8.6 billion living on the planet, have the exact same fingerprints, neurons, or cellular structure as another.

God is not wasteful, and did not suddenly become wasteful when Divine Intelligence created *you*. *You* are this unique, this special! Therefore, you have a special purpose and it is why you are living on earth at this time.

Spiritual and self-growth leaders have been teaching, for thousands of years, the incredible power each of us has at our disposal when we release fear.

Their wisdom is the reason we chose to focus book three on three chapters exerted from the Bible. When interpreted metaphysically, these three chapters reveal the profound and timeless wisdom used by such great spiritual teachers as Jesus and Abraham as they taught us about the crippling impact of fear, as well as how they individually practiced releasing it.

Their metaphysical teachings include how we can achieve spiritual unlimitedness by vanquishing the fears that enslave us. In turn, they encourage each of us to express our own spiritual uniqueness, as they had done; while accomplishing even greater things than they had achieved.

Spiritual leaders have consistently taught that our greatest enemies are the cocoons of fear we wrap around ourselves, because they cripple our beliefs, our thoughts, and our actions. In turn, those fears *transform our potential for unlimitedness - into limitedness*. While fear is initially experienced in your mind and emotions, it also triggers a strong physical reaction in your brain which severely limits your thinking capabilities.

When that happens, we are constrained, shackled, imprisoned, and fail to take advantage of the vast goodness our Creative Source has placed at our disposal. In other words, the promised bounty, the abundant harvest of goodness sits in the field always available, but unharvested; abundant, but unused.

Positive affirmations are important, but in themselves, are not sufficient. This is why many who use positive affirmations for prosperity fail to achieve the abundance they are requesting from the universe. The reason is that it makes no sense to be speaking positive affirmations aloud, while we have fears eroding our base beliefs which limit us from manifesting what we are requesting.

We have to also do the work, the practice, to have the divine manifestation take place. Like anything that is valuable, we have to *earn* what it is we desire.

This book, and the teachings from these great spiritual leaders are timeless. It will teach you how to achieve this outcome.

Book three is more than half-written. When finished, it will be professionally edited and prepared for publication. Advance orders can be purchased through richardfeller.com.

BOOK 4

This book is in the process of being outlined and written. It is anticipated it will be available in the later part of 2022.

It will focus on the turbulence being experienced in the workplace at the present time which will only continue to increase in the future.

Since the majority of people work and spend more than 30% of their lives in work efforts, and in organizations, this book will be centered on the type of organization needed for the future. It will include a discussion of the type of leadership and skills required for both management and non-management to survive in future marketplace turbulence.

Organizations with two or more people represent business, healthcare, education, non-profits, public servants including police and firemen, and government. Each will be addressed as part of the world of work. In business alone, more than half of all people employed by business work in organizations that have less than 100 employees.

Employees are changing jobs in record numbers. Each departure is a potential drain of intellectual capital or learned knowledge being lost to the organization that is being left behind, without even considering the financial disaster. The reason employees are leaving in droves is that they are searching for meaningful jobs with a purpose where they feel they can contribute and make a difference, and when they discover they can also gain financially by so doing, they are willing to gamble and make the switch. Obviously, their former position failed to meet those needs.

This book will build upon the metaphysical, business, education, administrative, and psychological knowledge taught in the fear-clearing trilogy and will describe the type of spiritual or self-actualizing organization required for the future.

It will also include examples of the types of business organizations the author helped to successfully economically transform in conjunction with the CEO and senior management team at two of the largest corporations in the world.

The book will be based upon the fact that leaders and employees in the process of self-actualizing themselves, as they lose the fear and personal limitations, they have previously carried within themselves, have the opportunity to become dynamos of new creative and innovative energy which in turn can be used to regenerate and revitalize the organization of the future.

This will be a fascinating and insightful read for both members of the work community as well as all those who are in the process of transforming themselves into becoming the masters of their own destinies.

ADDITIONAL SERVICES

BOOK SIGNINGS

The author is available for book signings. He will share a discussion about himself as well as a short applicable lecture if desired prior to the book signings.

LECTURES

The author conducts specialized lectures that are done concurrently with book signings. They are generally sixty to ninety minutes in length followed by open questions from the audience.

Generally, the lecture will proceed with book signings by a day or could also be arranged for the day following the signings. Potential subjects include:

A. How to remove your Fears while growing Metaphysically

B. How to integrate Spiritual and Metaphysical Principles to enhance business success

C. How to achieve Self-Actualization and Personal Mastery

D. Express your Self-Confidence and Self-Esteem

E. How to create Abundance in all ways

F. How to Enhance your Decision-Making comfortability

CONTACT

If you are interested in these services, please contact Jeff McCrehan at mccrehan@icloud.com to discuss the services in more detail and to be placed on the author's schedule. Please be advised that the author is frequently booked in advance and may not be readily available.

Made in United States
North Haven, CT
03 June 2022

19766931R10217